97

Managing Disability at Work

Improving Practice in Organisations

A

A

The Disability and Rehabilitation Series

Approaches to Case Management for People with Disabilities
Doria Pilling
ISBN 1 85302 099 0
Disability and Rehabilitation 1

Information Technology Training for People with Disabilities
Edited by Michael Floyd
ISBN 1 85302 123 7
Disability and Rehabilitation 3

Managing Disability at Work
Improving Practice in Organisations

Brenda Smith, Margery Povall and Michael Floyd

Disability and Rehabilitation 2

Jessica Kingsley Publishers *and*
The Rehabilitation Resource Centre, City University
London

Originally published in two volumes by the Rehabilitation Resource Centre, City University
Volume 1 ISBN 0 9513925 1 4
Volume 2 ISBN 0 9513925 2 2

First published in the United Kingdom in this edition in 1991 by
Jessica Kingsley Publishers Ltd
118 Pentonville Road
London N1 9JN

and
The Rehabilitation Resource Centre
Department of Systems Science
City University
Northampton Square
London EC1V 0HB

Copyright © 1991 the authors and the Rehabilitation Resource Centre

British Library Cataloguing in Publication Data
Smith, Brenda
    Managing disability at work: Improving practice
    in organisations. - (Disability and
    rehabilitation series)
    I. Title II. Povall, Margery III. Floyd, Michael
    IV. Series
    331.13

    ISBN 1-85302-123-7

Printed in Great Britain by
Billing & Sons Ltd, Worcester

Contents

Foreword to the 2nd Edition   11

Part I: Background and Introduction

1. Background to the Research   15

    Disability and Employment in Britain   15

    The Need for More Detailed Guidance   17

    Recent Developments   19

    The Rehabilitation Resource Centre Project   21

    Establishing a Training Programme   27

Part II: Improving Practice in 'Open Employment' Organisations

2. Disability Management Training Needs   31

    1. Recruitment and Selection   32

      Key Issues   32

      Knowledge, Information and Skill Needs   37

    2. Allocating People to Jobs, and Jobs to People   38

      Key Issues   38

      Knowledge, Information and Skill Needs   42

    3. Induction   43

      Key Issues   43

      Knowledge, Information and Skill Needs   46

    4. Training   47

      Key Issues   47

      Knowledge, Information and Skill Needs   51

    5. Building and Maintaining a Team   52

      Key Issues   52

      Knowledge, Information and Skill Needs   57

6. Working Relationships 58
    Key Issues *58*
    Knowledge, Information and Skill Needs *62*

7. Health and Safety 64
    Key Issues *64*
    Knowledge, Information and Skill Needs *67*

8. Motivating Staff 68
    Key Issues *68*
    Knowledge, Information and Skill Needs *70*

9. Fluctuating or Poor Performance 71
    Key Issues *71*
    Knowledge, Information and Skill Needs *74*

10. Career Development 76
    Key Issues *76*
    Knowledge, Information and Skill Needs *79*

11. Promotion and Transfer 80
    Key Issues *80*
    Knowledge, Information and Skill Needs *81*

12. Dealing with Organisational and Work Changes 82
    Key Issues *82*
    Knowledge, Information and Skill Needs *84*

13. Relations with Customers 85
    Key Issues *85*
    Knowledge, Information and Skill Needs *87*

14. Implementing the Organisation's Disability Policy 88
    Key Issues *88*
    Knowledge, Information and Skill Needs *89*

3. Priorities In Meeting Training Needs **91**

Who needs Training? 91

People with Disabilities 92

Immediate Supervisors 92

More Senior Managers 93

Specialist Advisors 93

Other Groups 94

How to Provide Training 95

4. Organisational Issues   **97**

People's Understanding of Disability   97

Whose Responsibility is the Management of Disability at Work?   99

The Role of Medical Staff in the Management of Disability   99

Communicating about Disability Issues   100

How can Communication be Improved?   102

The Role of Policy in the Management of Disability at Work   102

Why should Organisations have a Policy
    with Resources allocated to Disability Issues at Work?   104

5. Summary of Recommendations for Improving Practice in 'Open Employment' Organisations   **106**

Training   106

Disability Policy   107

Part III: Improving Practice in a Sheltered Employment Organisation

6. The Research in Remploy   **111**

The Views of Staff on the Need for Managers and Supervisors
    in Remploy to have Greater Knowledge of Disability Issues: 111
    Productivity   111
    Safety   111
    Discipline   112
    Employee Development   112

Situations requiring Disability Management   112

The Need for Knowledge about Certain Types of Disability   117

The Need for Information about an Employee's Disability   119

7. Developing Training in Remploy   **122**

Staff Views on Training   122

Meeting the Training Needs of Managers   123

Meeting the Training Needs of Supervisors   124

Meeting the Training Needs of Other Groups   125

Meeting the Training Needs of all Employees   126

8. Organisational Issues in Remploy   **128**

    Introduction   128

    Personnel Procedures   128

    Safety Procedures   130

    Aids and Adaptations   131

    Health and Welfare   132

9. The Wider Implications of the Research in Sheltered Employment   **135**

    Introduction   135

    Organisations providing Sheltered Work   135

    Other Organisations   136

Appendices   **138**

    1. Collaborating Partners   138

    2. Types of Disability of People Interviewed   139

    3. Additional Types of Disability those Interviewed in Open Employment Organisations Reported having Experience of Managing   140

    4. Other Organisations Visited or Consulted   141

    5. Profiles of the 'Open Employment' Organisations Researched   142

    6: REMPLOY   148
        Mark Daymond, Director of Personnel at Remploy

References   **153**

Acknowledgements

We would like to thank all the organisations, and their representatives, who have collaborated with us to help plan and carry out this research. We are especially grateful to the many people with disabilities and their colleagues whose views and experiences form the basis of this report.

We would also like to acknowledge here the contribution of the Manpower Services Commission (now TEED) and the Department of Education and Science, without whose financial support no work could have been undertaken.

And finally we must thank John Hill, Robert Levy and Sue Peachey whose skills have made it possible for us to produce this book.

Foreword to the 2nd Edition

The work described in this book was carried out during 1987 and 1988. Since that time, we have been developing and running a training programme at City University called 'Disability Management at Work'. It is designed to meet some of the needs we identified in our research and which we describe here. Our courses at the University have been attended by over a hundred employing organisations, including thirty-five local authorities, fifteen government departments, and a range of private companies and other organisations. We have also developed in-house training for several employers, and are currently preparing a training manual on disability management at work.

Our experience of developing and running these courses has convinced us that the meeting of training needs and organisational issues addressed in this book are as pertinent now to the improvement of employment opportunities for people with disabilities as they were when our original work was carried out. We are also convinced that the effective management of disability at work must take account of the central role played by the individual with the disability.

With the publication of the Department of Employment's Consultative Document 'Employment and Training for People with Disabilities', it has become apparent that there is likely to be considerable restructuring of the services available, including an expansion of private and employer-based services. This will bring with it a greater need for disability-related training and new groups of people requiring such training, including service providers and those giving employment and training advice to people with disabilities.

While this book is not in itself intended as a training manual, it will, we hope, alert both employers and service providers to the key areas which need to be addressed, as well as their own disability management training needs and those of their staff.

The authors
Rehabilitation Resource Centre
April, 1991

Part I

Background and Introduction

Chapter 1

Background and Introduction to the Research

Disability and Employment in Britain

Government policy in Britain today is still largely based upon a number of critical assumptions about disability and employment which were set out in the report of the Tomlinson Committee, published at the end of the Second World War (Tomlinson, 1943). The recommendations of this committee, which were embodied in the 1944 Disabled Persons Act, resulted in:

- the establishment of a Quota Scheme whose aim was to ensure that at least 3% of the workforce, of all non-governmental organisations with over 20 employees, were registered disabled people

- the setting up of a national network of industrial rehabilitation units to rehabilitate disabled people

- the development of a service to help disabled people find employment.

The Tomlinson Committee also recognised that some people might be so severely disabled that travelling to, or working in, an ordinary job would be impossible. They therefore proposed that the government should provide sheltered employment in industrial workshops for such people.

As many other writers have pointed out (for example, Wansbrough and Cooper, 1979) the Tomlinson Committee was very much concerned with the problems of ex-servicemen, disabled by physical injuries incurred on active service. The Committee also had to find acceptable compromises between the interests of trades unions and employers (Bolderson, 1980). Their recommendations were therefore flawed right from the start and this can be seen most clearly in the way both the Quota Scheme and the services failed to meet the needs of those with disabilities resulting from a psychiatric illness.

The 1944 Act was nonetheless an impressive piece of legislation and represented a tremendous advance in furthering the employment prospects of people with disabilities. The problem lies in the way in which, in spite of a multitude of policy reviews over the last forty years, very few significant changes have been made either to the Quota Scheme or to the rehabilitation and resettlement services (Cornes, 1982). What is even more surprising is that the assumptions underlying the Tomlinson Committee's recommenda-tions continue to provide the context for debate regarding any possible future changes.

Three key assumptions can be identified:

- that most people with disabilities, once they have been rehabili-tated, are no different in employment terms from other people. Not only are they just as productive, but their needs are no different and they can, and should, be treated in exactly the same way as other employees. In other words their disabilities will not significantly handicap them at work

- that only a very small proportion of disabled people cannot be rehabilitated in this way, but will continue to be significantly han-dicapped as far as employment is concerned, and so will require sheltered employment

- that the handicapping effects of a disability can only be reduced by rehabilitating the individual with the disability, rather than, for example, by modifying the work environment.

The importance of such assumptions in shaping policy can be seen when one contrasts the British situation with that of other countries (Kulkarni, 1981). Thus, in West Germany, there is a recognition that severely disabling condi-tions are not only common but that they should, as far as possible, be accommodated within ordinary (open) employment. This results in a Quota Scheme, in which employees who fail to meet their quota are charged an 'equalisation levy', so that any competitive advantage they might gain, from not employing their quota of disabled people, is cancelled out. In West Germany there is also a tremendous emphasis placed on vocational training, which is seen as helping to counteract the competitive disadvantage experi-enced by someone with a disability.

Although both the assumptions underlying government policy, and the policies themselves, have continued to be remarkably resistant to change, the last few years have nonetheless seen some significant developments. Not the least of these has been the increased emphasis on what the Manpower Services Commission described as 'positive policies'. Rather than compel employers to employ their quota of disabled people, the Commission has argued that they should be encouraged to adopt more enlightened policies

16

and practices. To help them do this it published a Code of Good Practice, containing a comprehensive and fairly detailed set of suggestions as to how employers could improve the opportunities of both prospective and existing employees with disabilities.

To support this initiative the Commission also re-organised its resettlement services. Disability Advisory Service teams were set up to help employers implement better policies and practices and make them more aware of the assistance available from the teams themselves and other rehabilitation and resettlement services.

The Need for More Detailed Guidance

The Code of Good Practice and the development of the DAS teams undoubtedly represent an important advance. There is a growing awareness, though, that employers and people with disabilities need more. The Code, while excellent as a basis for developing better policies, does not provide the kind of detailed guidance that is needed if organisations are going to translate worthy statements of intent into relevant practices - with regard to recruitment, selection, etc. - on the ground.

Perhaps more importantly, the Code - like Tomlinson - fails to acknowledge that difficulties can arise not only at the recruitment stage - getting people with disabilities into employment - but also once they are in the job. Once this is recognised we have to answer some difficult questions:

- what are the reasons for any difficulties which do arise?

- could they be avoided, and if so, how?

- if a difficulty cannot be avoided, how might it be successfully overcome?

One crucial issue to be tackled is whether the problem results directly from the disability, for example does the individual have a 'special need' relating to the disability which is not being met? Or are there other factors causing or aggravating the problem which require an organisational rather than disability-related approach for its solution?

Unfortunately, the answers to questions such as these do not exist in a comprehensive and systematic form. This is partly because remarkably little research has been carried out into the employment experiences of people with disabilities. Such knowledge and skills as exist tend to be 'locked up' in the heads of individuals who have either direct or indirect experience of working with a disability.

Any difficulty arising at work will also be perceived and interpreted differently by each individual, depending on whether it is the person with the disability, their employer or colleague, a professional adviser or service provider. For example, a study of the employment experiences of people with schizophrenia, carried out some years ago by one of the authors of this report (Floyd et al, 1983), found that the problems they encountered at work were, in many instances, very different from those the professional workers assumed to be important. Thus, anxiety about their own work performance turned out to be a major reason for leaving, or not returning to, a job in which they were in fact performing quite satisfactorily. What seemed to be needed here was more adequate feedback on performance. Lacking such insight, it was all too easy for rehabilitation workers and employers alike to believe that the individuals concerned simply lacked 'motivation' to work, a simplistic explanation of a very complex phenomenon. The inadequate interpretation of a problem such as this will inevitably present an obstacle to finding possible solutions.

Other complicating factors in this regard are:

- the tendency to treat people with disabilities at work as a homogeneous group, but distinct from the rest of the working population. This overlooks the wide range of types and degree of disability, the uniqueness of each individual (e.g. their abilities, aptitudes and preferences), and the fact that any member of staff can become disabled.

- the assumption that once a person with a disability has been recruited and any necessary aids provided or adaptations made to the premises, no further assistance or support will be required. This direct consequence of the assumptions underlying Tomlinson, discussed earlier, is also questioned by findings of the above study (Floyd et al, 1983). These suggest that employers and colleagues, as well as people with disabilities, may have need of advice, support or information, and this need can arise at any stage of employment. An extreme example cited is that of the colleagues of a person with schizophrenia who suffered remorse and self-reproach when their colleague jumped from a car park roof, sustaining multiple physical disabilities.

- the 'laissez-faire' attitude of many employers in relation to disability, for example their belief that a person with a disability, once recruited, is responsible for 'fitting in' to the organisation or workgroup, and that the goodwill of colleagues will surmount any potential difficulties. As the example above indicates, goodwill alone may not be enough, and advice or information may be required by others in the organisation, for example supervisors and managers, personnel and welfare officers, and occupational health staff, as well as people with disabilities and their immediate colleagues.

The need is for more detailed, concrete guidance, targeted on specific groups in organisations such as those mentioned above. This provided the starting point for our investigation. Before describing how this was initiated and carried out, it will be helpful to outline briefly some of the other ways in which a variety of organisations are also attempting to grapple with these issues.

Recent Developments

One of the most significant responses to the needs outlined above has been the appointment, by a number of large organisations, of staff with a special responsibility for improving the employment opportunities for people with disabilities in their organisation. These staff are most commonly found in central government, where they are known as Departmental Disabled Persons Officers (DDPOs), and in local government, where they are sometimes known as 'disability officers.' Several large organisations in the private sector, especially financial and insurance companies, have also appointed staff with a similar remit.

A number of organisations have attempted as well to build upon the Code of Practice and formulate their own set of policy statements and guidelines for good practice. Thus the Civil Service has published 'The Employment of Disabled People Code of Practice' and the Trades Union Congress and Confederation of British Industry have also published guidance for their members.

Another important development has been the way in which many large organisations have integrated disability into their equal opportunity policies, along with gender and race. Other important initiatives include:

- the advertising of job vacancies in publications targeted on disabled people (for examples, RADAR's 'Contact' and the Spastics Society's 'Disability Now')

- Lambeth Borough Council's controversial, but ultimately successful, campaign to employ their quota (3%) of registered disabled people

- the establishment of the London Boroughs' Disability Resource Team, with a staff of nearly 20 employees (most of them with disabilities) to provide training information and guidance for the boroughs. (For a more detailed and comprehensive survey of recent initiatives of this kind, see Doyle, 1987).

Mention should be made too of the growing awareness in North America of the importance, for employers, of developing more coherent and appropriate approaches to the prevention, and management, of disability in their organisations. It is also worth noting in this regard that much of the impetus for the emergence of disability management as a key area in North America comes from the increasing costs, to organisations, of 'permanent health' or 'disability' insurance. As in West Germany these costs provide a financial incentive to organisations to examine more carefully ways of maintaining the health of their employees and preventing, and managing better, any disabilities that they experience. It seems likely that, with this kind of insurance becoming more popular in Britain, we shall see similar pressures developing here.

Finally a brief reference should be made to one other recent innovation that promises to become an important aspect of future provision. This is the Sheltered Placement Scheme (SPS). During the last few years the number of SPS placements has grown enormously and, following a recent review of the future of sheltered employment by the Department of Employment, there is every likelihood of continuing growth in this area. Originally sheltered placements were conceived primarily in terms of a means for providing opportunities in open employment for people with disabilities who cannot be as productive as other workers. The Shaw Trust, though, which now employs more people with disabilities in SPS placements than all other organisations combined, has demonstrated that an important aspect of the 'sheltered' concept is the provision of ongoing support for their employees. MENCAP, too, have shown, with their 'Pathways' scheme, how important such support can be in maintaining people with more severe disabilities in employment.

The Rehabilitation Resource Centre

The large increase in the number of SPS places has not been the only important development with regard to the provision of sheltered employment. During the last few years Remploy, which provides sheltered employment for over 9000 people with severe disabilities in its factories, has been obliged by the government, which subsidizes its operations, to become a more viable organisation. This has meant, amongst other things, adopting more modern and appropriate personnel policies and approaches to training. One area of particular concern was the absence, in Remploy, of any training of its supervisors and managers aimed at making them more aware of the special needs of their employees and how these can be met. Initially this area was identified as involving 'disability awareness training.' In the course of subsequent discussions with the Rehabilitation Resource Centre staff, though, it was recognised that a more appropriate term would be 'disability management training.' Awareness training, it was pointed out, was already being developed - for example, by the London Boroughs' Disability Resource Team - in order to make people more aware of their prejudices towards people with disabilities and to reduce disability-related discrimination in employment. The emphasis in 'disability awareness training' is thus on changing people's attitudes.

In Remploy, what was needed in addition to increased awareness of disability issues were the knowledge and skills to manage disabilities at work on a day-to-day basis. It was also pointed out that this emphasis on the practical management of disability was needed not just by Remploy's managers and supervisors (many of whom themselves have disabilities), but also by everyone in the workplace who is involved in disability management. This of course includes each person who has a disability, as they are primarily, and in some ways uniquely, responsible for its management. Thus any training developed was seen as encompassing this aspect, and the term 'disability management' should not be taken as implying, as in so much of rehabilitation, something which is done to, or for, people with disabilities by those without disabilities.

In order to meet the needs of both Remploy and other 'open employment' organisations in this area a major investigation of training needs was undertaken by the Rehabilitation Resource Centre to identify the knowledge and skills that were needed in the management of disability at work. It was decided that the investigation should, in the first instance, include employees with physical disabilities, and that the training needs associated with psychiatric and learning disabilities merited a separate study. It was also decided to concentrate the study initially on the knowledge and skill needs of managers and supervisors.

A project was set up with funding from the Manpower Services Commission and Department of Sciences PICKUP programme, and from Remploy. Several other organisations, besides Remploy, agreed to become 'collaborating partners' and to contribute in a variety of ways towards the project.

Three of our collaborating partners, in addition to Remploy, made it possible for us to carry out research into their training needs and interview staff in their organisations. These were all 'open employment' organisations, one in the public sector and two in private. (A complete list of collaborating partners and the members of the Steering Committee is given in Appendix 1).

Our research into carrying out the research began with a one-day workshop, to which were invited experienced staff from the organisations collaborating with us. Meetings were also held with a number of other individuals with both an academic and a practical involvement in this area (see Appendix 4). Issues raised in both the workshop and the meetings provided the basis for designing a series of semi-structured interview schedules which varied according to whether the person interviewed:

- was with or without a disability

- had or did not have supervisory responsibilities

- had special organisational responsibilities (e.g. personnel, training).

Each interview was designed to touch briefly upon many aspects of the individual's working life, both in their current employment and elsewhere, as well as their experiences of disability management both inside and outside employment. Where appropriate, health issues were also discussed. As the main area of interest was the day-to-day management of disability at work, each interview allowed time for concentrating on areas in which the informant had considerable experience, for example recruitment, training or teamworking. Other employees with whom the individual worked (i.e. in the same reporting line) could then be asked about the same issues, where appropriate, to compare perceptions.

Our primary aim throughout the research was to identify training needs in relation to the management of physical and sensory disabilities at work. The main emphasis was the analysis of managers' and supervisors' training needs and finding ways to meet these. In addition, we recognised the importance for effective disability management of both the organisational context and the other people involved.

A total of 70 interviews were carried out in the four employing organisations. Thirty eight of the people interviewed had disabilities, of whom four were interviewed as 'non-disabled' but revealed a disability at interview. These people have not been included in the 'disabled' figures in the table below.

Job levels of people interviewed, giving distribution of those with disabilities in "open" and "sheltered" employment organisations

Job level	Number interviewed	With disability	With disability in 'Open' employment	'Sheltered' employment
Senior Manager	7	1	1	-
Middle Manager	13	2	2	-
Supervisor/ Trainee Manager	14	8	2	6
Assistant Supervisor	8	8	-	8
Employee without supervisory responsibility	15	15	6	9
Personnel Officer	3	-	-	-
Training Officer	2	-	-	-
Medical/Welfare Officer	6	-	-	-
Other	2	-	-	-
Total Interviewed	70	34	11	23

Within each organisation, as far as possible, interviews were carried out with people in the same reporting lines, i.e. a person without supervisory responsibility, their assistant supervisor and/or supervisor, their line manager and their senior manager. People with disabilities might be at any level in the reporting line. A list of their types of disability is included in Appendix 2.

In each organisation the people with disabilities were approached first and asked if they would be willing to be interviewed. If they agreed others in their reporting line were then approached. Organisations were asked to nominate people whose disabilities were representative of the types of physical disability most frequently occurring in the organisation. This criterion could be said to have been met in Remploy but in the other three organisations, where the numbers of employees with disabilities were much smaller, our request was interpreted in somewhat different ways with the result that our sample included:

- more people with visible disabilities, people using wheelchairs being most frequently nominated;

- the more severely disabled people in each organisation;

- those people with disabilities whose employment was regarded as either a 'success' or 'problematic' by their organisations.

Interviews were arranged in two of Remploy's factories:

- factory A, engaged in the manufacture of cartons and boxes

- factory B, engaged in contract packaging and assembly work, as well as carton and box manufacture.

In both factories everyone with a disability who was interviewed was engaged in manual work, with the exception of the production controller and his staff in factory A.

A third Remploy factory was also visited and the factory manager interviewed.

The figure below shows those who were interviewed and where they appear in the factory structure. It can be seen that as far as possible people within the same reporting line were interviewed.

Factory A:		Divisional Manager Manufacturing Manager Factory Manager Superintendent				Factory B:		Divisional Manager Manufacturing Manager Factory Manager Superintendent			
	S	S	S	S	S		S	S	S	( )	( )
	LH	LH	LH	LH			LH	LH	LH	( )	LH
	H	H	H	H H			H	H	H	H	

Key: S = Superintendent; LH = Leading Hand; H = Hand; ( ) = Not Interviewed

Note: All staff interviewed below the level of superintendent in both factories have disabilities, with the exception of two supervisors in factory B. The fact that all supervisors and leading hands interviewed in factory A have disabilities is somewhat atypical of Remploy generally, where approximately one third of supervisory staff are people with disabilities who have been promoted.

Other staff interviewed included:

- factory doctor, safety officer, chief first aider, other first aiders (both factories)

- production controller and staff, (factory A)

- homeworkers' organiser and welfare and assessment officer (re-tired), (factory B).

It is important to stress that because of the way the interviewees were selected, our investigation was not able to cover all types of disability, and certain disabilities were discussed by interviewees who had indirect, rather than direct, knowledge and experience of their management at work. (Appendix 3 lists the additional types of disability which those in open employment reported having experience of managing.) In particular, issues of multiple disadvantage have not been addressed. It is hoped that our future work will extend to cover these aspects, as well as the management at work of psychiatric and learning disabilities.

In every case a very detailed interview note was prepared and analysed systematically. This analysis then formed the basis for preparing reports on the disability management training needs within each of the four organisations. These reports were subsequently discussed with staff in the organisations concerned. In turn they have been used to prepare this publication, which aims to make our findings more widely available and to provide a basis for the development of training programmes relevant to the needs that have been identified.

Following the introductory Part I, the book is divided into two further parts.

Part II: *Improving Practice in 'Open Employment' Organisations*
Profiles of the three 'open' employment organisations in which interviews took place are presented in Appendix 5. Two are in the private sector and one in the public sector. In each organisation, primarily white-collar work is undertaken. In each organisation fewer than 1% of the total workforce was known to have a disability.

In all three organisations the co-operation of the personnel or equal opportunity function was first enlisted. One organisation provided a list of people known to have disabilities. A number of people were then invited to be interviewed on the basis that their disabilities were, as far as possible, representative of the types of disability most frequently occurring in the organisation and because they were doing a range of different jobs. Although the other two organisations were asked to apply the same criteria, in one of them people with disabilities were selected by them either because theirs was thought to be a 'success story' or because ongoing problems were being experienced. In the other organisation selection of interviewees was done by a member of the medical staff who approached *'people who would not misinterpret the purpose of the interview.'*

In each organisation, once a person with a disability had agreed to participate, others in their reporting line were asked if they were willing to be interviewed. The figure below shows those who were interviewed in the

Organisation A

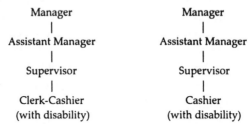

```
      Manager                    Manager
         |                          |
 Assistant Manager          Assistant Manager
         |                          |
     Supervisor                 Supervisor
         |                          |
   Clerk-Cashier                 Cashier
  (with disability)          (with disability)
```

Organisation B

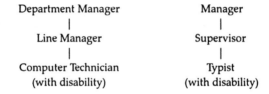

```
 Department Manager              Manager
         |                          |
    Line Manager               Supervisor
         |                          |
Computer Technician               Typist
  (with disability)          (with disability)
```

Organisation C

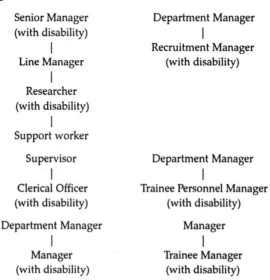

```
    Senior Manager           Department Manager
   (with disability)                |
         |                  Recruitment Manager
    Line Manager             (with disability)
         |
     Researcher
   (with disability)
         |
   Support worker

     Supervisor            Department Manager
         |                          |
   Clerical Officer      Trainee Personnel Manager
  (with disability)          (with disability)

 Department Manager              Manager
         |                          |
      Manager                 Trainee Manager
  (with disability)          (with disability)
```

three 'open employment' organisations, where people with disabilities appeared in each reporting line, and the kind of work they were doing.

Other staff interviewed included:

- personnel, training and welfare officers in organisation A

- personnel and medical staff in organisation B

- equal opportunity, training and medical staff in organisation C

Part III: *Improving Practice in a Sheltered Employment Organisation*

There are two reasons for having separate parts. Some of the disability-related training needs in 'open' and 'sheltered' employment organisations are different. Therefore the most appropriate ways of addressing them are different too. Secondly, the investigation of training needs in sheltered employment was carried out in one organisation, whereas the open employment findings are based on interviews in three organisations. In addition, while work carried out in Remploy is manual, in the other organisations white-collar work is undertaken, so that comparison is not valid.

Part 2 does not identify training needs in individual organisations but attempts to reach general conclusions from the findings in all three organisations.

Part 3 is essentially the report presented to Remploy. The discussion of certain organisational issues has been omitted at their request, as these were not felt to be widely applicable.

Establishing a Training Programme

As a result of the project a training programme was set up in 1988 by the Rehabilitation Resource Centre at City University, in order to assist employers wishing to improve practice in their own organisations. With a generous grant from the Nuffield Provincial Hospitals Trust, a training manual is also being developed. These training courses and materials are designed to meet some of the needs we have identified. We hope they will assist others wishing to develop training in disability management at work and to integrate disability aspects into more general training, such as management and personnel training and work organisation.

Part II

Improving Practice in 'Open Employment' Organisations

Chapter 2

Disability Management Training Needs

An early finding in our investigation was that interviewees found it extremely difficult to define their own training needs, in spite of strongly held feelings that training would be helpful to them in the management of disability at work. It was therefore found productive to explore with them situations which they identified as difficult, and to discuss with them the disability management factors involved.

In this chapter we present the situations which were discussed. They have been arranged according to the aspect of work to which they relate, for example 'recruitment and selection', 'job allocation', 'induction', etc. Each of these work aspects contains three sub-sections:

- key issues associated with the work aspect, each illustrated from the interviews. Text set in small capitals indicates examples of particularly good practice

- the information needed by those responsible for managing such situations

- the skills involved in managing such situations.

The knowledge, information and skill requirements which are identified, together comprise the 'disability management training needs' relevant to the situation.

1. Recruitment and Selection

Key Issues

(a) An organisation's recruitment and selection policies and methods may inadvertently discourage potential recruits with disabilities from applying for jobs and/or present barriers to their selection.

> 'After I lost my sight I gained a degree in sociology and a postgraduate diploma in personnel management. I then applied for any kind of personnel work. Out of over a hundred applications I only got one interview. Some firms replied, some didn't even bother. Knowing how Personnel works it does not really surprise me. The main priority is 'How can we short list?' They look at all the applications first to see who they can get rid of. Some companies will bring in the first 20 applicants and put the rest in the bin. Some look at qualifications and take the highest. Some see disability and throw it out straight away, irrespective of anything else.'

Recruitment Manager with visual disability

(b) People with disabilities may not apply for jobs because they have had frequent rejections in the past. They may need special encouragement to apply.

> Malcolm was just turned 40 when he lost the use of his legs as the result of an accident which also resulted in incontinence. As a wheelchair user he found that access difficulties and the lack of suitable toilet facilities close to his workplace made continuing in his existing clerical job impossible. A large number of unsuccessful applications to similar small firms advertising clerical vacancies further reduced Malcolm's already damaged self-esteem: 'When you become disabled you go into the disabled world. You go to clubs and so on where you meet other disabled people. I met several people with disabilities working for Councils, and they suggested that I apply direct to public sector organisations. That's how I got this job.'

IN ORDER TO ENCOURAGE APPLICATIONS ACTIVELY, ONE ORGANISATION HAS A POLICY OF INTERVIEWING EVERY APPLICANT WITH A DISABILITY WHO APPLIES. ANOTHER ORGANISATION HAS ESTABLISHED A SPECIAL SUPERNUMERARY SCHEME TO INCREASE THE NUMBERS OF PEOPLE WITH DISABILITIES IT EMPLOYS.

SMALL CAPITALS DENOTE GOOD PRACTICE

(c) Ignorance and prejudice may wrongly exclude the selection of people with disabilities.

> *'I would expect someone with a disability to definitely have more sickness absence. Disabled people are weak and can't do things - they need more consideration.'*

Manager, Computer Programming

(d) Advertisements and job descriptions, which contain details of the tasks involved and the working conditions, give people with disabilities a much better idea of whether or not they might be able to do the job. Analysing the job requirements in detail also makes it easier to select the best candidate.

> John, an accounts clerk who is paraplegic, was accepted for a job in a large open-plan work area. He is located near the entrance, the rest of the work area being overcrowded with desks, filing cabinets or cupboards with double doors. *'There is not enough room to open the double doors from a wheelchair, and some files are too high. There are too many people and too much furniture around, so I cannot even get around the office. I depend on people bringing me files. When they are busy they cannot be expected to do that. It's all so dependent. Disabled people need some independence, but I cannot have it in this set-up. I would never have taken the job if I had known. Most able-bodied people do not understand our need for independence.'*

> *'I was accepted as a trainee manager in a restaurant. I had to work at a large open grill and I found co-ordination difficult. You had to work at a very high speed, cooking lots of items in quick rotation. There were quick manual movements and co-ordination necessary. I thought I would not have credibility as a manager training other people to use the grill if I could not do it myself, so I resigned after two and a half months.'*

Trainee Manager in Industrial Relations
with visual disability

(e) Application forms containing many questions about health and disability issues do not normally assist in selecting the best candidate, and may unjustifiably exclude people with disabilities.

> *'I see job applications and I always check on the medical history section. If it's patchy you obviously think twice about offering them*

a job, particularly if they are getting older. I'm looking for people who can stand a lot of pressure, who can deal with a lot of work and different things at the same time. If there was any indication they couldn't take the strain I wouldn't take them.'

Manager of Computer Department

One manager suggested that his organisation includes a detailed health section in its standard application form because the conditions of the company pension scheme would preclude anyone considered a 'high risk' from joining. He thought this might be a reason why few people with disabilities are employed in the organisation.

The opposite point of view was expressed by a senior manager in another organisation: *'EVERYONE BELONGS TO THE COMPANY PENSION SCHEME. THERE ARE NO EXCLUSIONS AND NO WEIGHTINGS. It's really no excuse for any medium-to-large company to say that their disabled staff cannot be included in the scheme, because company schemes are based on a mixture of risk levels.'*

(f) The work experience and education of people with disabilities may be unusual. Unnecessarily rigid or restrictive selection criteria may exclude suitable candidates.

People who have attended special schools or whose education has been interrupted by spells in hospital may lack formal educational qualifications. In addition, selection techniques used may be inappropriate in their standard format, as one officer with a visual disability found: *'I failed the psychometric tests because of the speed factor. The tests themselves were not too difficult. I got a very high success rate in what I managed to get through, I was told, but I just did not manage to get through enough because of the size of the print.'*

(g) Selection procedures should be well planned to ensure that interviewers or panel members with disabilities participate fully.

'I once interviewed with Colin for a clerical officer for his team. Not everyone is initially aware that he is blind until they see the dog. We decided in advance which areas we would each cover. The panel was chaired by a woman from central personnel who was very good AND MADE SURE THAT WE WERE ALL INVOLVED IN THE INTERVIEW.'

(h) Interview premises, which are difficult or impossible for candidates with restricted mobility to reach, or interview arrangements which pose difficulties for a person with restricted hearing or sight, may also pose problems for other candidates.

Panel interviews, especially those involving several panel members, present considerable difficulties for people with communication disabilities (e.g. missing the first few words a person says if you are lip-reading; having to maintain eye contact with a questioner while making a response and then rapidly focus on a different questioner). Such interviews were also described as particularly stressful by people with other types of disability, as well as by people who are not disabled.

(i) Interviewers should take account of candidates' relevant skills, experience and the knowledge they have acquired other than in paid work.

Gill, a typist with a hearing disability, is thought by her manager to be capable of routine copy-typing work only. She teaches lip-reading to people with hearing at evening classes. She does not disclose this skill at work as she feels it would be thought to be irrelevant. However Gill would like the opportunity to teach others office skills. Amongst the organisation's clerical trainees are other people with hearing disabilities, but there is no internal provision for meeting special training needs. There is, therefore, a training need which is not currently being met and a resource to meet that need which is not currently recognised, both of which could have been ascertained at interview.

(j) A little medical knowledge can be a dangerous thing. People with the same disability will have very different capabilities.

'I am OK with close work as long as I have direct light on the paper I am working with. When I applied for jobs after I passed my law degree I started giving the information about my sight in a separate letter, and I was getting an awful lot of rejections. My colleagues were getting interviews. I am very shortsighted and I have astigmatism. When I did get the occasional interview they led me to believe they had doubts about my sight and then I started to wonder. For example, I was asked: 'Did you see the programme on the television last night about the cricket ball that bleeps?' I had

mentioned that I play cricket. It was assumed that I played in a blind team. That is not so. There was, therefore, a preconception that I could not do the job, that I was blind. The question was nothing to do with my ability to do the job. How do they think I got my law degree?'

Trainee Manager in Industrial Relations
Department, with visual disability

(k) A visit to the workplace can help candidates decide whether this presents any practical problems for them.

'Before I started the manager said I could choose which of the two branches in the town I wanted to work in, so I had a look at both of them. In the other branch the counters were higher and there was a pillar just inside the door making it difficult to manoeuvre the wheelchair. The car park wasn't as convenient as this one either. The manager must have realised how much better it would be for me here because he said he thought this branch would probably be better, but IT WAS GOOD TO BE ABLE TO SEE FOR MYSELF.*'*

Cashier with paraplegia

An officer with cerebral palsy worked in a large complex of offices with reasonable wheelchair access. When his department was closed, he was relocated to another section. He accepted the relocation as he welcomed the challenge of a different kind of work. He then discovered that his new section was housed on the third floor of an annex with no lift.

(l) With individual determination and possibly aids and adaptations, a person who is regarded as a most unlikely candidate may become a valued employee.

Mary, a school leaver who is paraplegic, was recruited as a supernumerary. Within a few months she had become a member of the organisation's establishment staff and was undertaking supervisory responsibilities. She is now seen as having management potential, and is a highly valued member of staff in her department. However, not everyone recognised Mary's potential on recruitment: *'The assistant manager admitted afterwards that he had assumed I would not be able to do the job. I used to get that at college as well. My test results at college surprised some people when they were so good. Then they started*

SMALL CAPITALS DENOTE GOOD PRACTICE

to accept me. Just because you can't walk, some people think you are mentally disabled as well. I think a good manager gives you a chance to show you are good at the job. I would like to get to management eventually, as high as I could.'

Knowledge, Information and Skill Needs

Managers and others involved in making decisions about recruitment and selection need to know:

Knowledge and Information

1. What the organisation's policy is on the recruitment of people with disabilities (both registered and non-registered), and whether any extra encouragement can be given to people to apply, e.g. an agreement made to interview all applicants with disabilities.

2. What external sources to contact and where to place advertisements in order to attract suitable applicants including those with disabilities.

3. What questions it is appropriate to ask at interview about the work implications of a disability and the individual's needs and preferences.

4. Where to get expert advice or help with assessment should it be difficult to assess an applicant's suitability for a particular job or potential for other jobs.

5. To what extent restructuring of jobs to meet an individual's needs is allowed or encouraged by the organisation, and what possible implications there may be for other employees, e.g. if tasks are reallocated.

6. Where to get information both within and outside the organisation on the availability and suitability of aids and adaptations and sources of funding for such equipment.

Skills

1. How to analyse jobs and specify requirements which do not unwittingly exclude suitable candidates.

2. How to make interview and selection test arrangements which do not pose difficulties for people with disabilities, whether known or unknown.

3. How to interview candidates in such a way as to obtain maximum relevant information without causing embarrassment or offence.

4. How to assess the suitability for a job of a person with a disability whose education, formal qualifications and/or previous work experience may not conform to usual selection criteria.

5. How to organise selection panel procedures in advance and to enlist the co-operation of all concerned, in order to ensure that anyone with a communication disability who is involved in the selection process has the opportunity to participate equally with other panel members.

6. How to recognise organisational barriers to the recruitment and selection of people with disabilities, and how to identify ways in which these barriers can be removed or reduced in ones own organisation.

7. How to find out, before the interview, if a candidate has any special needs, e.g. access for a wheelchair, a signer, or speech facilitator, and how to meet these.

8. How and when to obtain additional advice on the practical consequences at work of a particular type of disability.

9. How to interpret medical information received about a particular individual in the light of job demands and the existing working environment.

10. How to choose appropriate selection tests which are free from bias against people with disabilities.

2. Allocating People to Jobs, and Jobs to People

Key Issues

(a) People with many different kinds of disability, including people with severe disabilities, are doing a wide range of work, including jobs with high pressure and skill levels.

> Included among the more senior staff of the four organisations researched are: a recruitment manager who is blind; a production controller who has paraplegia; a deputy director and an educational welfare officer both of whom have restricted limb usage; a researcher who has cerebral palsy; a supervisor who is both deaf and without speech (and who has in her workgroup people with learning disabilities whom she trains); and a computer programmer with muscular dystrophy. However, in all the organisations there were

SMALL CAPITALS DENOTE GOOD PRACTICE

individuals who were unaware of anyone with a disability in a position of responsibility.

(b) It is important to look at the individual components of jobs and ways of overcoming potential obstacles rather than making negative assumptions about an individual's disability precluding them from doing the job.

> *'I have no experience of disability outside of work. My experience of working with one disabled person would make me look at other disabled applicants very carefully in terms of what I thought they could achieve. If I thought they were borderline I wouldn't consider them for this department. We push people hard in the field we are in. A lot of my people are on night call on a voluntary basis and you wouldn't expect a disabled person to do that. And I wouldn't touch mental problems with a barge pole because those people would never be able to take the pressure.'*
>
> Manager of a computer department

When a line manager had a nervous breakdown, it was thought unlikely that he would be able to continue in a management role. However, following discussions with the person concerned, he was successfully moved from line management to a management job in the organisation's administrative centre. A senior manager explained the reasoning behind this decision: *'It was decided to remove as much as possible of the stress element from his job.* THE MOVE ENABLED US TO REDUCE PRESSURES ON HIM WHILE RETAINING HIS EXPERIENCE AND EXPERTISE.' To the individual, the retention of his grade and status was an important factor in aiding his recovery.

(c) Redistributing a few of the tasks involved in different jobs amongst staff members may make it possible to employ a person with a disability on a job not otherwise seen as suitable, while enabling members of the workgroup to develop new areas of expertise.

> *'There have been changes in office practices as a result of having two people with disabilities working in this office, including one of the team leaders who has a visual disability. He probably does more than his fair share of the telephone work and almost all the interviewing.* THE MEMBERS OF HIS TEAM DO MORE ORGANISING OF INDUCTION COURSES AND GOING THROUGH APPLICATION FORMS THAN WOULD NORMALLY BE THE CASE. THEY ALSO VET JOB ADVERTS [BEING PLACED

BY THE OTHER DEPARTMENTS] WHICH THEY WOULDN'T NORMALLY DO. MY RESPONSIBILITY IS TO ORGANISE THE WORK SO THAT IT GETS DONE BUT WITHOUT MAKING ANYONE FEEL UNDERVALUED.'

Manager of recruitment department

(d) Aids and adaptations (many of which are both simple and cheap, while others are provided free) can assist a person to do a job from which they might otherwise be thought to be precluded.

One large organisation is producing a chart of the aids used by its employees who have disabilities WHICH INCLUDES INFORMATION ABOUT ADAPTATIONS MADE TO ENABLE MAXIMUM ADVANTAGE TO BE TAKEN OF NEW TECHNOLOGY. IT IS INTENDED THAT THIS CHART WILL BE CIRCULATED TO RECRUITERS AND TO NEW PEOPLE WITH DISABILITIES WHO JOIN THE ORGANISATION.

(e) The person with the disability is an excellent, probably your best, source of information on their own capabilities and the management of their disability. They may well know what aids and adaptations are available and suitable, or where to obtain such information.

Gill, who is a typist with a profound hearing disability, is a teacher of sign language at evening classes. She has developed a set of guidelines for her hearing pupils on how to facilitate lip-reading. Her colleagues do not know of her teaching experience and have not asked her for advice or information about special needs resulting from a hearing disability. Gill would be glad to give such guidance if asked, but does not feel able to offer it, although she feels both she and her colleagues would benefit at work from their greater awareness of these factors.

Amrit is a college-leaver recruited as a clerk-cashier. As she uses a wheelchair her manager took action before she started work to improve access both to and inside the workplace: *'I contacted the DRO [Disablement Resettlement Officer] at the local Job Centre and was given the name of the DAS [Disablement Advisory Service] Manager. He visited the branch and told me what assistance was available. We had interior ramps put in so Amrit could start work, and then we had the toilet done.* WE CALLED AMRIT IN BEFORE THE WORK STARTED SO SHE COULD SEE WHAT WAS BEING PROPOSED. *She was able to make suggestions, and in fact she reduced*

SMALL CAPITALS DENOTE GOOD PRACTICE

the work that was proposed. She suggested that rehanging the inside door of the toilet was not necessary, provided a lock was fitted on the outside door. She was also able to anticipate difficulty reaching high level files, which she will need to do when she progresses in the job. The MSC [Manpower Services Commission] is providing her with a special chair which will raise her to that level, and they have also paid almost the whole cost of the adaptations.'

(f) The contribution to a work group offered by a person with a disability can be unique and invaluable but is often overlooked.

A typing pool undertakes a range of work including audio- and copy-typing, word-processing, and telephone reception duties. One member of the pool does copy-typing only, as she has a hearing disability. The supervisor and manager have very different views of the value of this contribution. The supervisor considers this narrow role to be *'a definite asset to the group, as most people prefer doing audio-work, and copy-typing is not very popular'*. However in the manager's view this typist *'is not doing a full job'*.

(g) It is important to utilise the skills and experience of a person with a disability in a meaningful way by allocating them 'real' work.

Jim, who is paraplegic and uses a wheelchair, worked for many years in a finance department where he developed considerable expertise in figure-work. When that department was closed Jim was transferred to a personnel section because wheelchair access is good there. After some weeks his new line manager has still not clearly defined Jim's job, saying he feels that a person with a mobility disability needs extra settling-in time. Jim fears there is no real job for him here: *'They created a job for me which has not really got going. I do not think it will ever be satisfactory full-time work. It is so frustrating because I do not feel as if I have got a proper job to do.'* The manager acknowledges that there is not likely to be much call for figure-work skills in his section.

(h) Inappropriate and unrealistic placements can reduce employment opportunities for other people with disabilities.

> *'Being disabled myself I think I have a more realistic awareness of other people's disabilities. I realise they can manage and let them get on with it. But one particular person I inherited was over-graded by his previous employers for the appointment he was given. His case was mismanaged from their point of view. He was in a highly placed post which I think was a token placement. Before he came here he had already had one unsuccessful transfer. They didn't really check if he could do the job at that grade. He is intelligent, but slow in communicating and writing, and has to have a support worker to act as his interpreter and aide as well as considerable additional supervision and management. He is someone with multiple disabilities who has been integrated, but at what cost? It was not originally intended he should work from home but [because the office facilities are not suitable] he is to all intents and purposes a home-worker who comes into the office about once a month. There are resource implications and he doesn't have all the equipment he needs at home. This is a very discouraging situation for others who are so severely disabled.'*

Senior manager of statistics department

Knowledge, Information and Skill Needs

Managers and others making decisions about the allocation of jobs need to know:

Knowledge and Information

1. Which of the jobs in the organisation are already being done successfully by people with disabilities which might appear to preclude them from such work.

2. Where to obtain information and advice within the organisation on special aids, equipment and other types and sources of assistance.

3. What the role of the various bodies and organisations involved with disability management are, and who can be contacted for what help.

4. How acceptable it is in the organisation to restructure jobs to accommodate people with special needs, and the procedures to be followed in authorising and implementing such changes.

5. An individual's failure at a job may not necessarily be related to their disability, and should not preclude another person with the same type of disability doing that job.

Skills

1. How to find out from the person with the disability their relevant experience, skills, and work preferences as well as tasks they may find difficult and ways of minimising any difficulties.

2. How to analyse jobs and their requirements in order to assess an individual's capability of doing them, and to enable the person to make a realistic assessment of their desire and ability to meet such requirements.

3. How to match a person's skills, knowledge, experience and potential to the requirements of the job.

4. How to relate similar examples from other organisations to ones own workplace.

3. Induction

Key Issues

(a) Taking time to prepare both the work group and the new person with a disability will make the first days easier for all and minimise the chance of later difficulties.

> A new recruit who was integrated into her department very smoothly and quickly, feels that THIS SUCCESS WAS LARGELY DUE TO THE MANAGER WHO SPOKE TO EACH MEMBER OF STAFF INDIVIDUALLY BEFORE HER ARRIVAL: *'The staff have been marvellous. There was no awkwardness at all. They had all been asked how they would feel about someone in a wheelchair working here for 5 days a week. They said "OK, as long as they can do the job." They expected me to do the work, and I appreciated that.'*

> *'If a new person was coming into this office now I would tell them that Sally needs to be touched to attract her attention, that she lip-reads and is happier using her own [modified] telephone. Also that she may need to be told if someone is waiting to see her. About Alan [who is partially sighted] I would say that he uses the telephone and does most of the verbal communication with visitors.*

When his reader is sick he asks anyone else in the team to go through his in-basket with him. Also he may ask to be taken to another part of the building. I would give the person adequate information so that things went smoothly and so that they wouldn't be afraid of the disability. The amount of information to give would have to be gauged according to the situation and to how much the person with the disability wanted disclosed, especially when it is an invisible disability. I WOULD ALWAYS ASK THE PERSON BECAUSE THEY MAY PREFER TO EXPLAIN IT THEMSELVES RATHER THAN HAVE IT DONE BY ME.'

Manager of recruitment team including people
with hearing and visual disabilities

(b) The standard induction procedure may need modifying, for a person with a disability may not have access to information about the organisation which other new employees obtain either formally or informally.

A person who uses a wheelchair works in a very large complex. Minor adaptations have been made to improve access in his immediate working environment, but he is unable to get to other areas, including those accommodating Personnel and other service departments where notice-boards containing information of general interest are located. He is therefore dependent on others volunteering such information. A person with a visual disability working in the same complex described similar difficulties, including lack of access to information about internal vacancies.

(c) A talk with the person with a disability before they join the workgroup will clarify what assistance, special provisions and aids are needed; and what information is to be given to whom, by whom, when and how, about the work consequences of the disability or any special requirements resulting from it.

'I was scared stiff of Gill for the first couple of weeks. I had seen her but I had never spoken to her. I had only heard her talking in the background. I was frightened, but she probably was too, hoping that she would be able to get her feelings across. I found I over-accentuated everything at first because I know I don't move my lips much when I speak. I then went home and found I was doing the same thing with my husband! People have different needs, and I think you have to work it out with the individual.'

Supervisor of person with hearing disability

In one organisation it is company policy that ANYONE ATTEND-ING A JOB INTERVIEW (WHETHER AN INTERNAL OR AN EXTERNAL APPLICANT) CAN VISIT THE SECTION IN WHICH THEY WOULD BE WORK-ING BEFORE DECIDING WHETHER TO ACCEPT A JOB OFFER. These visits usually last for about half an hour, and include an oppor-tunity to meet potential colleagues.

(d) A person joining an existing work group which includes a person with a disability may need advice to minimise any discomfort or apprehension.

In the organisation mentioned above where applicants for a job visit the section when being interviewed, A MANAGER WITH A VISUAL DISABILITY IS ABLE TO USE SUCH VISITS TO TELL THE PERSON IN ADVANCE ABOUT ANY ADDITIONAL TASKS THEY MIGHT BE ASKED TO HELP WITH, AND FOR THEM TO BECOME ACCUSTOMED TO HIS GUIDE DOG IN THE OFFICE.

'When new people come in there is a tendency for them to want to do things for Chris, but because she does most of the training of new staff they get used to her quite quickly. We recently employed an older lady. At first she couldn't get over the fact that we have a member of staff using a wheelchair. She kept on talking about it and telling her how wonderful she is, and I'm sure that must have embarrassed Chris.'

Supervisor of cashier with paraplegia

(e) Once induction has taken place, the person with a disability wants to be treated as normally as possible and may become demotivated or feel isolated if treated 'specially.'

In several cases managers and supervisors thought they were showing consideration, for example by giving people with disabilities less onerous tasks or by not involving them in discussion of work-related problems. The reaction from the employees was almost always negative: *'The impression I get is that I am treated like a child because I feel that decisions are made which involve me but which I am not consulted about. I am not treated with equal respect and consideration. They don't realise I've got brains until I lose my temper.'*

Typist with hearing disability

> *'I do not like to have special treatment at work. I want the same pressures as everyone else. I don't want them to say 'Don't give that to her', assuming I can't do it when I perfectly well can.'*

Clerical officer with paraplegia

Knowledge, Information and Skill Needs

Managers and others carrying out induction need to know:

Knowledge and Information

1. What issues should be covered when discussing with the person with a disability the job requirements and the needs of the individual and how they can both best be met.

2. What issues should be covered when briefing other group members e.g. layout of the room, extent to which they could or should adapt their work, how the new person wants to be treated, their access to any special equipment.

3. What issues to cover when briefing a person joining a workgroup which includes a person with a disability.

Skills

1. How to obtain relevant information about needs and preferences from a new staff member with a disability without causing embarrassment or offence, including discussing such matters with someone particularly sensitive about the disability.

2. How to provide a new staff member with detailed information about the organisation which a disability may make it difficult for them to obtain by other means.

3. How to encourage workgroup members to develop an awareness of an individual's abilities and special needs in order that they can help to integrate the individual into the group.

4. How to deal sensitively with staff fears and concerns.

5. How to provide additional information to an individual joining a group containing a person with a disability, if appropriate.

6. How to ensure that after induction a person with a disability is integrated into the workgroup as fully and speedily as possible.

7. How to supplement the existing induction procedure with additional information in order to provide details to which a person with a disability may not have access 'on the grapevine.'

4. Training

Key Issues

(a) People with disabilities require the same training opportunities as other staff, at appropriate stages of their career.

To ensure that all his staff obtain the training they require, a manager regularly discusses training provisions with his organisation's internal training function and assesses whether the needs of his staff are being met. HE PASSES ON THE COMMENTS AND OBSERVATIONS OF HIS STAFF ABOUT TRAINING, IN-CLUDING THOSE RELATING TO ANY SPECIAL NEEDS. One result is that when hotels are used as training venues for residential cours-es, ground floor rooms are selected for both training and, where appropriate, accommodation.

A computer programmer who uses a wheelchair is regularly sent on residential courses arranged by a large company supplying computer hardware and software, as his is such a rapidly changing area of work. THE TRAINING PROVIDERS ARE WELL EQUIPPED AND EXPERIENCED IN MEETING A RANGE OF SPECIAL TRAINING NEEDS WITHIN THEIR STANDARD TRAINING PROGRAMME. The individual's employers feel that the additional cost of providing a taxi to transport him to and from the training venue is well worth meeting. Their organisation benefits from his continually updated expertise, and from having the continuity of his services in a department which experiences rapid staff turnover.

(b) An individual with a disability may require special arrangements to be made in order that they can benefit fully from existing internal or external training.

In one organisation training is organised both regionally and centrally. One course which was organised by a region was to be held in premises without wheelchair access. A MANAGER

EXPLAINED THAT ONE OF HER STAFF WOULD NOT BE ABLE TO
ATTEND AND WHY. THE SAME COURSE WAS THEN ARRANGED BY
THE CENTRAL TRAINING FUNCTION, AS WELL AS BY THE REGION.
The central course was held in the organisation's own training premises, which have wheelchair access, and was available to any staff who were unable to attend the course in their
own region.

**(c) Where suitable adaptation cannot be made to an existing training
provision, alternative comparable external training is often available
which meets a special training need. People with disabilities may know
of sources and types of training suitable for them.**

The manager of a typist with a hearing disability did not
think she would be able to undertake word processing work,
and declined permission for her to receive training in this
area. She therefore attended evening classes for those with a
hearing disability to learn both word processing and book-
keeping: *'I had to go outside in my own time and get the qualifications by myself, and then they let me do the job.'*

**(d) People with disabilities may be particularly affected by inadequate
training provisions.**

A trainee cashier with a visual disability had her probationary period extended because her manager felt she had not
achieved an acceptable level of performance. Her supervisor
pointed out that the traditional informal training method of
'sitting by Nellie' when time allowed was proving inadequate since the introduction of computers, and particularly so
for someone with limited vision. Additional training time
and resources had been requested, but were so far refused.

**(e) Some people with disabilities will have developed their own (possibly
unusual) methods of learning new tasks. It is important to understand
what these are in order to assist in training, and to be able to check for
potential unexpected errors in task performance without inhibiting the
development of such self-training techniques.**

The trainee cashier mentioned above has developed her own
strategy for learning to use the computer, because of her
visual disability and the lack of aids. She has memorised the
sequence of the stages involved in opening and closing pro-

cedures, and follows these by listening for the different sounds made by the computer rather than by instructions appearing on the screen. When inputting or retrieving information, she looks at the overall shape of blocks of characters and where they appear on the screen, rather than reading individual letters or digits.

(f) A person with a disability may not have received the level of education and formal training of other staff members, and may therefore benefit from supplementary training.

A CORRESPONDENCE TYPIST WITH A HEARING DISABILITY IS GIVEN DAY RELEASE ONCE A WEEK BY HER EMPLOYERS TO ATTEND ENGLISH CLASSES, as the education she received at special school did not bring her language skills to an appropriate standard for dealing with business reports and correspondence, and her work requires her to correct grammatical errors made by the work originators.

(g) People attending training courses or using self-instructional material may have special training needs arising from a disability of which trainers are not aware. An assumption should not be made, therefore, that standard training materials and techniques are appropriate for all trainees.

Training is to be provided for all the members of a typing pool to enable them to use a new word processing system being introduced into their company. AS THE GROUP INCLUDES TWO PEOPLE WITH HEARING DISABILITIES, THE SUPERVISOR WILL TAKE STEPS TO ENSURE THAT THEY ARE FULLY ABLE TO PARTICIPATE IN THE TRAINING. For example, she will ask the trainer to stand in front of the group rather than behind when speaking, and will ask for written copies of all instructions to be made available.

(h) Training materials presented in different formats enable people with different kinds of disabilities to benefit from their use.

A training manager with a visual disability was particularly aware of the benefits of offering different kinds of training. As well as using internal and external courses and on-the-job training, THE ORGANISATION IS PREPARING DISTANCE LEARNING MATERIALS (which will eventually incorporate text, video and computer-based training) so that people can study at their own pace but with the availability of a tutor or counsellor. Individual learning will be reinforced by group discussions and seminars. The training manager is concerned that *'all material produced should be well and clearly presented. I am particularly aware of people who may have some disability.'* BY PRESENTING INFORMATION IN DIFFERENT WAYS, THE ORGANISATION WILL BENEFIT BY HELPING TO MEET THE TRAINING NEEDS OF ALL STAFF.

(i) A staff member with a disability who does not receive training offered to others in the department should be told why this is. They may assume incorrectly that this is because of their disability.

A computer programmer with muscular dystrophy said: *'Most of the people who are at the same grade as me have been on a junior management course. This is a one week residential external course. They said they would have to make special arrangements for me to go, that it wasn't impossible. But it didn't happen. If I had been mobile I probably would have been sent on the course to see if I had potential to be a manager. Maybe they decided it wasn't worth the aggro to send me.'* A colleague who did attend the course suggested that the criteria for being selected were having reached a certain grade and being in a managerial capacity, i.e. having responsibility for other staff. The person who did not go is at the appropriate grade but is in a specialist technical job rather than a managerial one. He has no responsibility for other staff.

(j) All staff may benefit from training or discussions to raise their awareness of disability issues.

In one organisation TWO OR MORE PEOPLE FROM THE SAME DEPARTMENT OR SECTION PARTICIPATE IN TRAINING OR DISCUSSIONS ABOUT DISABILITY ISSUES TOGETHER. This has been found to help in implementing and maintaining good practice.

The supervisor of a group which includes two people with hearing disabilities feels that training may help her avoid some difficulties of which she may at present be unaware. For example, she wonders whether misunderstandings sometimes arise because she has only attracted the attention of a lip-reader after she has begun to speak: *'They may miss a crucial word or two at the beginning of a sentence, such as 'Don't . . .'. We both may not realise that something has been missed.'*

SMALL CAPITALS DENOTE GOOD PRACTICE

BEFORE A YTS TRAINEE WITH A HEARING DISABILITY WAS DUE TO JOIN A DEPARTMENT, TWO MEMBERS OF THE DEPARTMENT ATTENDED A DEAF AWARENESS COURSE. They passed on information gained at the course to others. When the trainee started work she found that her new colleagues already knew how to avoid the main obstacles to lip-reading, and took steps to include her in both work and social interactions.

Knowledge, Information and Skill Needs

Managers and others considering training requirements and arranging training need to know:

Knowledge and Information

1. Whether internal training provisions are able to meet individuals' special training needs, if necessary with adaptation.

2. What training to meet special needs is available externally, and the cost implications.

3. What training on disability issues is available.

Skills

1. How to coach and provide on-the-job training.

2. How to make provision for additional time and/or assistance a person with a disability may require to develop a new skill.

3. How to recognise when an individual with a disability is not able to benefit fully from an existing training provision.

4. How to make explicit to a person with a disability the reason why they were not offered the same training as others in the department, and to involve them in selecting training more appropriate to their needs.

5. How to assess the training needs of individuals who may require special or supplementary training, and provide or obtain appropriate training.

6. How to consult people with disabilities in the organisation when planning training or discussions on disability issues, and to invite their active involvement as part of the training team.

7. How to assess the training needs of people who may lack formal educational qualifications or a range of previous work experience.

8. How to obtain special aids and equipment on short-term loan so that a person with a disability can assess their usefulness for the job during training.

5. Building and Maintaining a Team

Key Issues

(a) Members of an existing workgroup may have uncertainties or reservations about a person with a disability joining the group which could be dispelled by open discussion and involvement.

> An assistant manager was initially concerned when told that a person using a wheelchair would be joining the work group: *'I was a bit anxious at first because it is sometimes difficult to know what to say when somebody has a disability. For example, you don't know how far you can joke about the disability. I wanted to say things like 'If you eat too much you will buckle your wheels.' I am relaxing more now because she just laughs everything off.'*

(b) The person with a disability joining a workgroup will probably also have reservations and fears which could be allayed by discussion.

> Derek, who has limited mobility, was anxious about fitting in with new colleagues: *'I cannot get up steps. Sometimes I cannot get through doors. I worry about what would happen if we went out somewhere. I do not like relying on other people. If we were going out and I was afraid access might be difficult, I would just refuse the offer to go. At a staff dinner the men once carried me up and down the steps. They were very good, but I didn't like it.'*

(c) Maintaining independence can be of particular importance to a person with a disability, who may need encouragement to develop the ability to work in a team.

> The supervisor of a clerical officer who has paraplegia is conscious of that person's need to retain as much independence as possible while working within a team: *'I HAVE LEARNT NOT TO PANDER TO SOMEONE WITH A DISABILITY, TO LET THEM BE AN INDIVIDUAL BUT FULLY INCLUDED IN THE TEAM. I SAY TO OTHER*

SMALL CAPITALS DENOTE GOOD PRACTICE

STAFF "HELP WHERE YOU THINK YOU CAN, BUT DON'T MAKE A SPECTACLE OF IT."'

(d) People with different types of disability in the same workgroup may be able together to do a range of work which they would be unable to do individually.

A typing pool includes ONE PERSON WITH A HEARING DISABILITY WHO DOES COPY-TYPING, ONE PERSON WITH A VISUAL DISABILITY WHO AUDIO-TYPES DICTATED WORK, AND ONE PERSON USING A WHEELCHAIR WHO CAN DO EITHER KIND OF WORK. As the latter is not able to use a foot pedal she controls the audio-machine by hand. The work group, comprising five full-time and two part-time members, does all the typing for over a hundred people.

(e) Building a team which includes people with disabilities may require additional flexibility and co-operation on the part of all its members.

'As the line manager I assessed that Peter [who is blind] could do most of the duties demanded in the job. I think flexibility within the team and a willingness among colleagues are essential. You need to put it across that it is not necessarily more for people to do, but that they will have to do different things. You have to reorganise the workload. WITHIN THE TEAM YOU MUST NOT HAVE TOO RIGID IDEAS OF WHAT IS MY JOB AND YOUR JOB, BUT AS A MANAGER YOU HAVE TO CREATE THIS FEELING THROUGH THE TEAM.'

Manager of department including two people
with sensory disabilities

(f) Social and external events can be an essential extension of a group's work activities, and special thought may be necessary in order to ensure that a person with a disability is not excluded.

Two supervisors in different organisations stressed the importance of MEETING THE SPECIAL NEEDS OF A PERSON WITH A DISABILITY AS UNOBTRUSIVELY AS POSSIBLE WHILE ENSURING THEIR FULL PARTICIPATION IN GROUP ACTIVITIES: 'Staff meetings are held once a month for the staff in the two locations. They used to be held in alternate premises. Len was embarrassed because special arrangements were made to take him and his wheelchair to the other office which was not easily accessible. It seemed a whole performance for half an hour's meeting after work and everyone had to wait for us to arrive. We all agreed that we should hold all the staff *meetings here in the future because then we can start promptly, we can all get away quickly and there will be no need to embarrass Len.'*

'You have to think in advance about what might happen when people go on training courses and when we have staff socials. You have to make sure the facilities are OK beforehand for someone using a wheelchair and that training staff, for example, are advised. It is fine in our normal working environment because we are all very well adapted to it here. IT'S WHEN WE GO OUTSIDE THAT WE HAVE TO STOP AND THINK.*'*

(g) Once a person with a disability has been integrated into a team, group members sometimes forget or overlook any special needs they may have, and which may not continue to be met. This is particularly likely if the disability is not obvious or if the individual manages the disability unobtrusively and without involving others most of the time.

Once various adaptations had been made in the workplace and aids provided, a person who is not able to stretch upwards or climb steps was able to carry out almost all the aspects of his administrative job without calling on the assistance of others. However he is irritated, whenever new stocks of supplies are periodically delivered, to have to request that small quantities of the items he requires be shelved at an accessible level.

'Sometimes I get left out when the manager comes in and I am expected to ask afterwards what he has said. I am not automatically told what they are talking about. Also I get left out of conversations. I ask 'What are you talking about?' 'Nothing much', they say with a smile, but they've been talking for half an hour. They must have been talking about something. That's the biggest deafness problem, being left out.'

Typist with hearing disability

(h) Regular team briefings could provide an opportunity to raise and discuss disability-related issues as appropriate.

In one busy office telephones are shared between two people who work at desks facing each other with the telephones between them where the desks meet. This arrangement is inconvenient for one person using a wheelchair who is unable to reach his telephone because of the amount of paperwork on the desks. Part of his job involves dealing with queries from other departments, often by telephone. Whenever there is a call for him, someone else has to pick up the telephone and move it nearer him. If the telephone were permanently located within his reach, his 'sharer' would not have easy access to it. This situation causes minor irritation in the office. It is grumbled about, but never openly discussed.

In one department which includes a trainee with a hearing disability, staff meetings allow time for discussion of any difficulties experienced by the trainee or her colleagues. SIGN LANGUAGE IS GRADUALLY BEING INTRODUCED IN THE OFFICE, AND AT EACH MEETING A FEW NEW PHRASES ARE TAUGHT BY THE TRAINEE. The manager feels that this has improved the cohesion of the workgroup generally: *'Did you notice when you came into the office that everyone was busy signing? For the exchange of information Pauline is able to lip-read very well. But people in the office are starting to sign, with her encouragement, so that she is also able to socialise.'*

(i) The goodwill of colleagues towards a person with a disability in the workgroup may be insufficient if it is not accompanied by planning and, where appropriate, training, the provision of aids or other organisational assistance.

Before he had saved enough to purchase his own special vehicle, a computer programmer with muscular dystrophy had to be lifted from the taxi to his wheelchair and vice versa when his physical condition deteriorated. Colleagues who volunteered to do the lifting initially received no training, and one sustained a back injury as a result, for which the employers did not accept liability. TRAINING IN LIFTING WAS LATER GIVEN BY THE SAFETY OFFICER. One colleague commented: *'The Security people at the desk used to see Tony arriving outside and they would phone us up. People would look at each other . . . it was up to the ones who felt most conscientious. That's a thing of the past with his new car, but we should have had training earlier because we did do it better afterwards.'*

(j) Any changes in working patterns, the redistribution of work, or a change to physical arrangements in the workplace should be discussed in advance. People with disabilities and their colleagues may be seriously affected if such changes are made without consultation.

> A small typing pool includes two people with hearing disabilities, one who has almost no hearing and another who is deaf in one ear. The person who has no hearing in one ear prefers to work with no one on her deaf side, while her colleague prefers to sit in a corner facing all the other members of the workgroup *'so that I can see everything that is going on without having to move my head all the time or get left out of everything'*. Over a period of time the group has experimented with different seating arrangements in order to achieve maximum communication for everyone. THEY NOW HAVE A ROOM LAYOUT WHICH SUITS THEM ALL. The supervisor commented: *'People say our room looks like a knitting circle because we all face each other, but it's best for everyone that way.'* The typing pool will shortly be moving to a new building which is open plan, and this is causing concern to the members of the group as they fear they may not be able to organise their working area so efficiently. They have informally agreed that *'we will just have to look for a corner to take over.'*

(k) A person with a disability may misinterpret the intentions of a supervisor or colleagues if frank discussions between colleagues are not possible.

> Some people find themselves in the dilemma of not knowing whether to offer assistance or respect the person's need for independence. One manager with partial limb usage said: '[My disability] *has attracted a lot of sympathy and people have made allowances. I do not particularly want that. I want to be treated as me. With people who know I have got some disability I notice they go out of their way to say 'Can I open the door for you?' or offer to carry something. I would rather kick the door open. The ones who do not know treat me normally. They are either polite to everyone and open doors for everyone or they are not.'*

> Two large workgroups share an open-plan office where individuals make their own tea and coffee at a corner table. One person is assumed by his colleagues to bring a flask from home, as he drinks from a mug on his desk and they know

SMALL CAPITALS DENOTE GOOD PRACTICE

that he is unable to manoeuvre his wheelchair to the corner table. However the mug contains cold water which he obtains from a tap in the cloakroom. He feels hurt and angered that his colleagues do not offer to make him a drink, but will not ask them to do so. They know he likes to be as independent as possible, which they respect.

Knowledge, Information and Skill Needs

Managers and others responsible for building and maintaining a team need to know:

Knowledge and Information

1. What disability-related issues are of concern to a person with a disability joining or in a workgroup, which require outside assistance to resolve.

2. What issues concern prospective and existing colleagues of a person with a disability, which also require outside assistance to resolve.

3. What the person with a disability is willing for colleagues to know about the implications of their disability, and how they would prefer colleagues to be told, when and by whom.

4. What factors to bear in mind, in order to optimise group performance and communication, when deciding workplace and meeting layout (including seating and siting of equipment).

Skills

1. How to conduct open, frank and positive discussions with staff about their concerns relating to a potential or existing colleague's disability, and with the individual about their needs being met within the workgroup.

2. How to find out from the individual whether there are special considerations which should be borne in mind when arranging team activities outside the workplace (e.g. social events, group visits) and to ensure that these are met.

3. How to avoid conflicting priorities being set by workgroup members, and how to recognise when it is necessary for them to help each other to resolve such differences if they do arise.

4. How to communicate with group members so that everyone is included and understands, giving special attention if appropriate to those with communication disabilities.

5. How to resolve tactfully any difficulties in a workgroup caused by an individual's determination to prove themselves independent.

6. How to meet the needs of people with different kinds of disability in the same workgroup.

7. How to ensure that people with different kinds of disability are given the opportunity to contribute fully to the workgroup.

6. Working Relationships

Key Issues

(a) A manager or supervisor encourages good (or bad) practice amongst staff and others by their own words and actions, including those relating to disability.

> The supervisor of a workgroup, which includes a person who uses a wheelchair, TRIES TO ANTICIPATE ANY DIFFICULTIES IN ORDER TO PREVENT THEM ARISING. For example, before the members of the group participate in any outside activity, the supervisor checks with the venue that there is easy wheelchair access. One hotel being used for a meeting had revolving doors at its front entrance, which the hotel offered to remove temporarily. The supervisor realised that such action would embarrass her colleague, and arranged that they would all use a side entrance.

> *'I have occasionally had to pull people up as far as disability issues are concerned. Someone put the word 'tolerance' in a memo regarding a trainee with a disability.* I TOLD HIM THAT THAT WASN'T THE APPROPRIATE APPROACH. YOU TOLERATE FAULTS, NOT PEOPLE WITH DISABILITIES. *'*

> Equal opportunity manager

(b) It is easy to make incorrect assumptions about the capability of someone with a disability, or about the implications of the disability, which can lead to inappropriate action or assistance.

> A trainee manager who has diabetes used to be a storekeeper and was keen to extend his responsibilities. However, whenever he made a suggestion or tried to enter discussions about

SMALL CAPITALS DENOTE GOOD PRACTICE

making improvements his line manager was dismissive. When the storekeeper asked the reason for this negative attitude, the line manager advised him that the departmental manager had given instructions that the storekeeper *'should not be encouraged to get into any heated discussions because of my condition . . . that it would bring on an attack. I found it demoralising because that was not an issue for me. It didn't stop them giving me heavy duties, which could have been more of a problem.'*

One organisation fitted an audible signal in its lifts so that people with visual disabilities would know when the door opened. This has not helped one blind employee who said: *'I don't need a signal to tell me when the door is open because I can feel it and hear it. What I need is a signal which will tell me which floor we have reached.'*

(c) Whilst there are some common factors in the management of similar types of disability (e.g. those affecting mobility), each person is an individual with needs and preferences of their own.

A workgroup contains two people with hearing disabilities. One person, who is deaf in one ear, prefers to work and sit at meetings with no one on her deaf side. The other person, who is profoundly deaf, prefers to sit facing all her colleagues as she relies on lip-reading. She described an earlier experience: *'Another deaf girl came some years after me. She came to learn word-processing, but she couldn't cope and was asked to leave. The word-processing was too complicated. She had been given a little training but not enough, and she wasn't given a chance to try another job. Later I asked if I could transfer to that word processing job. I was told 'Deaf people can't do that job.' I was furious. I told them not to regard all deaf people as the same. We all have different levels of ability. I then went to evening classes for the deaf to get the qualification to prove to them that I could do the job.'*

Typist with hearing disability

(d) A manager or supervisor needs not only the understanding but also the skills to deal with the misconceptions of employees and others (e.g. customers) about disability .

One manager said he would not want to give additional responsibilities to people with disabilities: *'The disabled are weak and cannot do things. They are really like the very old in my opinion, and need to be treated with extra consideration.'* The supervisor of a person with a disability in this department would like guidance in how to get round his manager's negative attitude.

'It's easy to forget with Pam that she has a disability. A new young girl who came into the workgroup has found it difficult. It took her two weeks to include Pam when asking if the other people in the group wanted a drink from the machine.'

Supervisor of person with hearing disability

(e) A person with a disability may value assurances that their special equipment, behaviour or appearance is not causing difficulties or embarrassment to others.

'Sometimes I know I make a noise and don't realise it because people tell me, for example, to take my hand off the repeat space bar on the electric typewriter.'

Typist with hearing disability

A manager who is blind has no way of knowing whether his appearance is causing embarrassment unless colleagues point this out to him: *'I would like them to tell me if I have spilt my breakfast down my tie, but would they?'*

(f) Some people with disabilities may be reluctant to ask for information or help which they think might highlight their special needs and adversely affect their opportunities.

A cashier who is paraplegic does a great deal of on-the-job training of new recruits and agency staff. Her workstation, which is at the counter dealing with customers, is not wide enough to accommodate a chair next to her wheelchair. *'When I train other people they have to sit behind me or stand next to me, which is probably not ideal as they may not be able to see everything properly. I don't want too many changes made just because of me though, because it looks so awful.'*

(g) Communication difficulties arising from sensory disabilities can lead to misunderstandings.

Two people with visual disabilities described misunderstandings which arose because they were unable to see the facial expressions of colleagues and had taken jokes seriously.

A senior manager commented that a line manager who is blind *'is only able to communicate in a very direct way, and it can rub people up the wrong way.'*

The supervisor of a deaf typist took some months to discover that if she shouted her mouth was distorted and her words could be incorrectly interpreted by a lip-reader.

(h) The active involvement of a manager or supervisor with a disability in the selection of their own staff will provide the opportunity to discuss with potential colleagues their own work preferences and unusual demands resulting from special needs.

Paul is manager of a recruitment section. Much of his work involves interviewing applicants. He supervises a team of four and a YTS trainee. Because Paul has a visual disability, a personal reader assists him with paperwork for part of each day. When the reader is not available Paul calls on the services of other members of his staff ' . . . *to do jobs which are not strictly part of their job description. I LIKE TO BE ON THE INTERVIEW BOARD IF SOMEONE IS GOING TO BE WORKING FOR ME. I talk to them about the team as a whole and they are also told that on occasions I will turn to them when I have not got my reader with me to find me telephone numbers and get me information and things like that.'* Additional tasks may also involve accompanying Paul to different locations and bringing interviewees from the reception area to Paul's immediate working area. The senior manager of the department suggested that a new person who was not properly briefed before joining Paul's section might find it irritating to be asked every so often what they are doing by a supervisor who *'is not able to look up and see them doing the filing.'*

(i) Those who find ways to discuss disability-related issues openly are better able to prevent difficulties arising and deal with any which do arise.

THE SUPERVISOR OF A YTS TRAINEE WITH A HEARING DISABILITY ATTENDED A HEARING AWARENESS COURSE BEFORE THE TRAINEE'S ARRIVAL. As a result she felt able to prepare the members of the workgroup and to avoid some of the difficulties which might have arisen: *'You must not assume that young people can sign . . . or wish to in the office. i also learnt about the sheltered life of many young deaf people and the need for extra confidence giving . . . the cultural shock when they start work . . . that their understanding may be different . . . that people who are lip-reading may feel very tired by the end of the day, constantly using their eye muscles to see what people are saying.'* The course gave her the confidence to encourage open discussion of such issues, with the result that the trainee had been happily integrated and was now teaching everyone in the office how to sign.

A trainee cashier with a visual disability was thought by her manager to be producing sub-standard work. Her medical report had been sent by the eye-specialist to the personnel function, which had approved her recruitment. Neither the manager nor his staff was told in detail about the work implications of the visual impairment, or about visual aids which would have enabled her to do the job more efficiently. The trainee, a school-leaver, did not feel able to discuss her difficulties with the manager. Her supervisor was sympathetic, but lacked both knowledge and authority to take any action.

Knowledge, Information and Skill Needs

Managers and others responsible for establishing and maintaining good working relationships need to know:

Knowledge and Information

1. The stereotypes and misconceptions about disability can cause more difficulties for people than their disabilities.

2. There is a continuum of disability to non-disability. A disability can be visible or not apparent, it can result in differing degrees of handicap

SMALL CAPITALS DENOTE GOOD PRACTICE

which will be reduced or increased by the working environment, and it may or may not be related to illness.

3. The rates of sickness absence of staff with and without disabilities, in order to dispel pre-conceptions that a disability will necessarily result in higher sickness absence.

4. The achievements of other people with similar types of disability both inside the organisation and elsewhere, especially those carrying out jobs which may not seem immediately suitable and of how this has been achieved.

Skills

1. How to dispel misconceptions about disabilities, including setting an example by ones own words and actions.

2. How to find out from the individual relevant correct information about the implications of a disability (if appropriate and without being intrusive).

3. How to talk tactfully to an individual about their behaviour or appearance if it causes embarrassment to others, and to a colleague if their behaviour toward a person with a disability is inappropriate.

4. How to ensure that secondary factors which may be associated with having a disability are minimised in the workplace.

5. How to compensate for secondary factors which may be associated with having a disability (e.g. lack of self-confidence, narrow range of work experience, previous limited training opportunities).

6. How to incorporate special aids and equipment into the workplace with minimal inconvenience to others, and ensure that as far as possible adaptations to existing equipment made for a person with a disability will enhance rather than limit its use by others.

7. Health and Safety

Key Issues

(a) Often people with disabilities can most easily identify aspects of the work environment affecting the safety of themselves and their work.

A NEWLY RECRUITED WHEELCHAIR USER WAS INVITED TO VISIT THE WORKPLACE TO POINT OUT ANY POTENTIAL HAZARDS OR OTHER DIFFICULTIES: *'She told us what the potential problems might be by us asking her and going round with her. She was very honest and knew her own capabilities.'*

'There are a couple of things I am concerned about. I have asked for something to warn me when the fire alarm goes off because I can't hear it. It's outside the office. And I'm also concerned about safety outside. I can't hear cars coming up behind me. There are no paths in the car park, so I've nearly been knocked down several times.'

Typist with hearing disability

(b) The health and safety implications of the same type of disability may be quite different for different individuals. One person may be able to do a job quite safely when another could not.

Epilepsy can take a number of different forms. For most people seizures are well controlled by medication or only occur during sleep, and they are able to drive and undertake most types of work at all levels. For a minority there are serious safety implications which prevent them, for example, from working at heights or with unprotected machinery. However in many cases individuals with epilepsy are refused jobs involving any perceived risk, whatever form their disability takes and irrespective of whether they are legally permitted to drive.

(c) The special safety and evacuation procedures which may need to be set up for people with disabilities seldom cause problems in organisations, and can heighten the safety consciousness of all staff.

One organisation in which staff are involved in handling money has a ruling that at least two members of staff must be present when premises are unlocked in the morning. The

64

procedure requires that one person remains outside while the other enters to check the premises. The same procedure is followed in a branch where a person with restricted mobility is employed: 'MICHAEL CAN BE ONE OF THE TWO WHO OPEN UP, BUT NOT THE ONE WHO GOES INSIDE TO CHECK. *He can wait outside and count for the necessary number of seconds before calling the police if the person who has gone in has not come out again. It's for his own safety and the security of the branch.'*

IN A LARGE BUILDING WHERE A NUMBER OF PEOPLE WITH DIFFERENT DISABILITIES WORK, EACH SECTION HAS DESIGNATED INDIVIDUALS WHO ARE RESPONSIBLE FOR THE EVACUATION OF PEOPLE WITH RESTRICTED MOBILITY AND SENSORY DISABILITIES IN THE EVENT OF AN EMERGENCY. The Safety Officer feels that these arrangements have made all staff more safety conscious.

(d) Managers' and supervisors' concerns about an individual's safety may result in them overprotecting the person and refusing them useful work experience.

'The word processing worries me. He is an extremely accurate typist and seems to know by feel if he has made an error. He can see the screen, but sometimes he has to look closely at it. I think the flicker and colour on the screen might make it more stressful for him, but he has never said that it does. I have to tell him to stop doing it as I feel it is a strain.'

Manager of trainee personnel manager
with visual disability

(e) Expensive adaptations may not be necessary; many aids exist which enable people with different types of disability to work safely.

Since flexitime has been introduced it is no longer possible to ensure that a typist with a hearing disability always has company in the office. As she is unable to hear the fire alarm bell, which is in the corridor, A WARNING LIGHT IS BEING FITTED NEAR HER WORKSTATION. THIS WILL FLASH WHENEVER THE FIRE BELL RINGS. THE SYSTEM WILL GIVE HER GREATER SECURITY AND INDEPENDENCE.

In many banks and building societies, cashiers sit on high stools in order to be at a convenient level for attending to customers. However, in one organisation false floors have been constructed on the cashiers' side of the counters which raise staff above ground level. An assistant manager explained that 'THIS HAS BEEN DONE IN ALL OUR BRANCHES SO THAT THE CASHIERS CAN SIT ON ORDINARY CHAIRS. THIS AVOIDS THE BACK PROBLEMS WHICH BESET PEOPLE ELSEWHERE. IT ALSO MAKES IT EASIER FOR US TO EMPLOY PEOPLE WHO USE WHEELCHAIRS. AND BECAUSE OF THE PERSON USING A WHEELCHAIR IN THIS BRANCH, WE HAVE A RAMP UP TO THE FALSE FLOOR INSTEAD OF STEPS, WHICH HAS MADE IT EASIER AND SAFER FOR EVERYONE.'

(f) Employees may generally be ignorant of safety regulations and procedures, increasing the hazards for all staff.

In all the organisations there were individuals who expressed uncertainty about safety regulations and procedures, including emergency evacuation. One wheelchair user said he thought that in an emergency his colleagues would *'just throw me over their shoulders and run.'*

(g) The return to work after a long absence caused by illness or injury needs to be carefully managed to avoid unnecessary stress both to the individual and colleagues.

'We have arranged shorter working hours for people. There are two people at present working three days a week as a result of heart attacks. This was decided jointly between the senior manager, our company doctor, the individuals themselves and their own doctors. WE HAVE TOLD THEM 'IT DOESN'T MATTER WHEN YOU GET IN BUT JUST COME IN ON MONDAYS, WEDNESDAYS AND FRIDAYS.' THEY MAY START LATE AND GO HOME EARLY. THERE IS A GRADUAL BUILD UP FROM THERE ON. *They are kept on their full time pay levels for pension purposes, and they get their normal salaries. One individual turned up for work five weeks after having had a heart attack. The nurse was horrified and now we have a rule that she has to see people who have been away after serious illness to agree that they are well enough to return to work.'*

Personnel manager

(h) It may be possible to find ways of adapting safety and evacuation regulations.

> *'I think some of the safety regulations need reconsidering. For example if the spring strength for the fire doors were set at the legal limit, neither Greg, who has muscular dystrophy, nor the girls in the office would be able to get through them. One person broke their hand after the springs in the doors were tightened. And if they enforced the fire regulations to the limit neither Greg nor anyone else using a wheelchair would be employable here. We are bending the law in collaboration with the fire brigade by agreeing that if there is a fire we will leave Greg at the top of the stairs and the fire brigade will carry him down.'*
>
> Manager, Computer Unit

Knowledge, Information and Skill Needs

Managers and others responsible for health and safety need to know:

Knowledge and Information

1. Who in the organisation to contact about safety regulations and their implementation and any concerns about safety.

2. What general and special evacuation procedures exist.

3. Where to get necessary medical and other advice on the possible safety implications of a disability.

4. Where to get information on how to make special safety provisions (e.g. for those with hearing or mobility disabilities).

5. Where to get information and advice on meeting any special health or safety needs of an employee returning to work after a long absence.

Skills

1. How to find out from a person with a disability what the safety implications of the disability are in order to plan the best way of ensuring a safe working environment without overprotecting the person concerned.

2. How to recognise and minimise potential hazards in the workplace.

3. How to inform all concerned with regard to general and special evacuation procedures.

4. How to ensure there is cover in the case of absence of any designated person with a specific safety responsibility.

5. How to find out tactfully from an individual returning to work after a long absence due to illness or accident, what their capabilities are and what adjustments or help, if any, they need.

6. How, if a person is temporarily or permanently unable to do their job, to assess their new capabilities and decide how best to integrate them back into the organisation (e.g. by redistributing tasks, minimising the effects of loss of status and confidence, and dealing with possible adverse reactions from colleagues).

8. Motivating Staff

Key Issues

(a) People with disabilities sometimes feel that the additional effort they make to do their job or improve performance is not recognised. This is particularly demotivating when a manager is not aware of their full contribution and regards them as 'not doing a complete job.'

> Gillian, a college leaver with a visual disability, was recruited as a trainee clerk-cashier. Her probationary period was extended because her manager is not satisfied that she has achieved an adequate standard in different aspects of the job. He told Gillian that if she did not have a disability she would have been dismissed. Gillian and her supervisor both feel that this is an unfair assessment. Gillian has not been provided with the visual aids which would help her to do her job more efficiently. As she has to hold documents very close to her eyes in order to read them, she can be both slower and less accurate than other new recruits. Because of her errors the manager has not permitted her to receive more than very basic training as a cashier. She has received no training for the clerical tasks involved in the job. However the manager asks her to perform these tasks when he is short-staffed, and then criticises her standard of work. He has stated on her progress form that he does not consider Gillian to be capable of performing the job of clerk-cashier. He has suggested that she be employed as a cashier only, a job which does not otherwise exist in the organisation.

(b) The workrole played by a person with a disability may not conform to usual practice, for example a narrower range of tasks may be undertaken leading to specialisation. To increase the individual's motivation their specialist role may need to be formally recognised, or ways found to extend their range of expertise.

John is a computer programmer who has worked in the same department for a number of years. Muscular dystrophy makes it difficult for him to lift heavy reference manuals or stacks of computer printout unaided, so John prefers to work mainly at a computer terminal rather than deal with documentation. He also spends time visiting other departments to discuss and try to solve their computing problems. John has developed a specialist role as a *'trouble-shooter'*, and is frequently asked to sort out difficulties others experience with the computing systems he and his section develop. His section leader explained: *'John only does a fairly narrow range of work because he is an experienced member of staff and I can't throw very basic things at him. I try to give him more complicated and therefore more interesting work. That is a product of other people's lack of experience, not of John's limitations. I give him the jobs only he can cope with or where others would take too long.'* John's expertise, which is largely self-taught, is not recognised as such by the departmental manager, however: *'I don't think John will progress any further. He is not good at communicating, and is just passable in a technical role. If he wasn't disabled I would be much harder on him, so he has progressed further than a non-disabled person to be honest. In terms of breadth of work he is good at a very narrow field only. Others at his level would be doing a greater breadth of tasks. He doesn't deal with documentation or come in at night as the others do voluntarily. It's hard to convince him that he hasn't failed to progress further because of his disability.'*

(c) An individual's immediate supervisor is often much more aware of the extent of that person's contribution and workrole than are those in more senior positions.

The supervisor of a person with a disability may need to dispel misconceptions of senior staff about perceived limitations associated with the disability in order that the individual's contribution is more widely known and acknowledged, as the examples of both Gillian and John above show.

(d) Personal encouragement by a supervisor or manager may increase the motivation of a person with a disability, especially if their self-confidence is low.

> *'I do not think he has any limitations because of his disability. His only limitations are ones which could stem from his earlier disability experience . . . lack of confidence. He may say 'I cannot cope. I have bitten off more than I can chew.' You have to show him that he can cope.* I SHOW HIM HOW TO PRIORITISE AND ORGANISE SO THAT ALL THE PROBLEMS GET DEALT WITH. *He needs to learn to be calm and not panic. You have to build up confidence in your own judgement in this sort of work. We have discussed it in great detail, and he understands and agrees. I have deliberately given him difficult jobs which he has coped with admirably.'*

> Senior manager of trainee manager with visual
> disability in equal opportunity department

Knowledge, Information and Skill Needs

Managers and others responsible for motivating staff need to know:

Knowledge and Information

1. What tasks and level of performance each staff member achieves and whether they have any special workroles.

2. How the contributions of members of staff are perceived and whether they are acknowledged by those in more senior positions.

3. If a person performing a narrow range of tasks wishes and feels able to extend the range of work undertaken, and if so how to facilitate this.

4. Ways which exist in the organisation to reward effort and achievement.

Skills

1. How to encourage employees to talk about their work aspirations.

2. How to recognise and acknowledge the effort put in to achieve and maintain a good level of performance, and give credit for improvement in performance even if slight.

3. How to make those in senior positions aware of the contribution and achievement of a member of staff when these are not fully recognised.

SMALL CAPITALS DENOTE GOOD PRACTICE

9. Fluctuating or Poor Performance

Key Issues

(a) Inadequate or fluctuating performance may be related to inappropriate management of a disability (e.g. inadequate aids, training, communication), or to a health or medication problem.

> When a section leader with a visual disability was suddenly able to do less of his job than previously, his manager found it difficult to judge whether this was related to his disability. She then discovered that the reduced performance coincided with a change in his support service. The mature ex-journalist who had acted as his personal reader was replaced by an inexperienced school-leaver. The manager commented: *'I had not thought about the quality of the reader support, but I now realise the reader needs understanding and expertise both as a reader and also of administration and office practice. The experienced reader went and found things. The inexperienced reader says 'I do not know where to look for it.'*

(b) Staff with disabilities are sometimes given a narrow range of tasks which fail to use many of their abilities, and this causes boredom and frustration which can result in increased errors and poor performance.

> Redeployment to a job at a different level after illness can itself cause frustration leading to under-achievement, as one Personnel Manager explained: *'I do know of people being moved to less stressful work and to shorter hours, but it may not be successful. There are sometimes psychological problems. Lower level jobs require accepting a different status, and this may be very difficult to accept.'*

(c) A person with a deteriorating or fluctuating condition may well need help to retain maximum independence, privacy and dignity within the constraints imposed by work requirements.

> One organisation employs a nurse at each of the three locations where several hundred people work. The nurse is readily available to give confidential help and advice to all staff, who may have concerns about their own health or that of someone else: *'One manager contacted me as he was very concerned about a lady in his department. He said she didn't look*

at all well and had been shaking. He was concerned not to cause her stress, but he also felt I ought to know about it. I had never had occasion to meet this lady, but I telephoned her at a time the manager said she would probably be alone in the office, and to my relief she was. I explained her manager had said he was rather concerned about her health, and asked if she would mind coming to have a chat with me. She came down and told me that she had been undergoing tests at the hospital. She had been advised that they suspected multiple sclerosis, but it had not yet been definitely diagnosed. I felt that it was helpful to her to talk about it, and I reassured her that if anything was a problem to her in her job she should come to talk to me about it, and that we wanted to help as much as possible. I then reported back to her manager that there was a health problem which was being investigated, and that we needed to keep an eye on her and avoid giving her too much stress. He was concerned of course, but anxious to help and glad that I now know about the situation. I did not think it was appropriate to tell him that multiple sclerosis was suspected, but IF IT IS CONFIRMED AND I FEEL HE NEEDS TO KNOW I WILL ASK THE LADY'S PERMISSION BEFORE TELLING HIM. *I would not tell him without her permission, but sometimes you have to try to persuade people that it is in their own best interests for their manager to be told.'*

(d) An individual may be unaware of those aspects of their work causing problems for others because some people may be reluctant to criticise the performance of someone with a disability.

The manager of a person with Parkinson's Disease was reluctant to change the individual's work or responsibilities although these had become onerous as his health deteriorated: *'I had to arrange for someone to duplicate the work he was doing on the pretext they were checking it. This person played cricket professionally and had been a very active person. I suppose we held him on a pinnacle. It's difficult to start pulling the pinnacle away completely.'*

A receptionist with a hearing disability was a poor time-keeper. Her manager was reluctant to criticise her although she recognised that *'Pauline comes in late because she is not a good organiser. It has nothing to do with her being deaf. I may be more lenient because she is deaf and I know I should not be, but she has a lot of home problems and the managers generally are sympathetic because of it.'*

(e) The self-esteem of people with some conditions may be particularly low. It is important to recognise effort and give credit for improvement, even when the general trend appears negative.

In one organisation two people with heart conditions were working part-time but it was felt possible to keep them on full salaries. Both were nearing retirement age. One had returned to work too soon after a heart attack. THE EFFORT HE WAS MAKING TO RETURN TO WORK WAS RECOGNISED AND APPRECIATED. IN ORDER NOT TO EXACERBATE HIS CONDITION BY SENDING HIM HOME, IT WAS DECIDED TO AGREE TO FLEXIBLE WORKING. He works shorter hours, of his own choosing, and on three days a week only. The personnel manager said: *'You have to be very sensitive in terms of how such situations are managed and what is expected of the other people around.'*

(f) A manager or supervisor may have to explain acceptance of reduced performance, or unusual behaviour, to colleagues of a person with a fluctuating condition.

'You sometimes need to explain about a disability if the colleagues feel that the person is getting away with something which they themselves are not able to get away with. For example, resentment can build up if someone regularly comes in late and you may need to explain the reason for that. BUT I WOULD ALWAYS ASK THE PERSON CONCERNED FIRST, BECAUSE THEY MAY PREFER TO EXPLAIN IT THEMSELVES RATHER THAN HAVE IT DONE BY ME.*'*

Senior manager with several people with disabilities in her department

(g) Unpredictable or inappropriate behaviour at work may be linked to a fluctuating medical condition or to a change of medication.

'I think it is very important to be able to recognise a problem situation before it gets out of hand. When I was a new supervisor I had a situation with two women who were both going through hospital treatment. They used to wind each other up terribly. One eventually got transferred, although I tried to stop her going. If it happened again now I wouldn't let it go on for so long. I would send

them down to the nurse. They were probably both under a great deal of stress.'

Supervisor of typing pool

(h) Help, advice and training are available from external sources should an individual's deteriorating condition result in them being unable to continue in their present job.

Help and advice had been sought and received from various agencies by and on behalf of a number of individuals. For example, VOCATIONAL ASSESSMENT AND RETRAINING SERVICES HAD ENABLED ONE PERSON WITH A VISUAL DISABILITY TO MOVE SUCCESS-FULLY FROM FARM WORK TO PERSONNEL MANAGEMENT WHEN HE LOST HIS SIGHT, and the Disablement Advisory Service had provided information and assistance enabling several people to be retained or redeployed.

Knowledge, Information and Skill Needs

Managers and others dealing with fluctuating or poor performance need to know:

Knowledge and Information

1. What the organisation's policy is if an individual's inadequate performance is found to be related to a disability, or to a health problem.

2. When and how to intervene, or involve other colleagues, if an individual's deteriorating condition is affecting their work performance and causing concern.

3. What to do if symptoms of illness or stress are detected by oneself or colleagues, or reported by an individual about themselves.

4. Where help and advice, medical and other, is available within and outside the organisation for the person with a disability or a health problem, and for other staff involved.

5. What training is available within and outside the organisation, either to help an individual improve their performance, or to train them for alternative work.

6. What alternative working arrangements (either temporary or permanent) are possible in the organisation. What the criteria and procedures for recommending and agreeing them are.

SMALL CAPITALS DENOTE GOOD PRACTICE

7. What alternative areas of work exist in the organisation for an individual no longer able to perform their existing job to an acceptable standard.

8. Where an individual who has to be redeployed can get assessment, career guidance and retraining.

9. What the organisation's policy and practice are on early retirement on health grounds.

10. What alternatives to early retirement or dismissal exist within the organisation, and how to select the best option, both from the organisation's and the individual's point of view.

Skills

1. How to elicit tactfully from an employee possibly sensitive information on what work factors may impair the management of their disability or aggravate their medical condition.

2. How to find out from the individual what the consequences of organisational or other changes affecting their work may be to them, and how best to deal constructively with any resultant difficulties.

3. How to find out from the individual concerned and others what factors are contributing to reduced or inadequate performance.

4. How to minimise any problems for other staff arising from an individual's deteriorating or fluctuating condition e.g. by reorganising jobs, counselling individuals.

5. How to find out whether a health difficulty is temporary or likely to be long-lasting.

6. How to generate support mechanisms between staff working in high stress areas in order to minimise stress-related health problems.

7. How to recognise when it is appropriate to seek medical or other specialist advice if there is concern about an individual's performance or behaviour.

8. How to counsel an individual who, because of a deteriorating condition, has become unable to carry out their job satisfactorily.

9. How to assess the capability and potential of an individual who becomes disabled and has to be redeployed.

10. How to utilise available expertise, both inside and outside the organisation, when appropriate e.g. for assessment, counselling, career guidance.

11. How to relate medical information received to the work requirements of ones own department and the organisation as a whole.

12. How to set and agree realistic and reasonable goals and timetables and provide appropriate training for an individual to improve their performance.

13. How to monitor progress toward agreed goals and involve the individual in monitoring of their own progress.

14. How to determine whether alternative jobs which exist within the organisation will utilise an individual's capabilities as fully as possible whilst minimising the work implications of any disability or health problem.

10. Career Development

Key Issues

(a) Most people with disabilities will, like other staff, want the opportunity to extend the range of tasks they undertake, and aids and adaptations exist to facilitate this.

> The manager of a department has responsibility for over 150 people. Among his staff is a typist with a hearing disability who does mainly copy-typing. Because she does not do telephone or audio-work, the manager considers that *'she is not doing a normal clerical job . . . she doesn't do the whole job'*. He does not therefore consider her suitable for a more responsible role in the organisation. However, he acknowledges that *'often at night she is the only one here and I go in and give her any urgent piece of work to do. I take her in something at say 5.30 or 5.45 and she says 'Do you want that done today?' I always say 'It doesn't matter when it's done but I need it on my desk when I come in at 8.30 tomorrow morning.' It's always on my desk when I come in the next day, so I presume she must stay late in order to do it.'* The typist, Joyce, would very much like to extend the tasks she does, would like to acquire new skills and hopes for more responsibility. She was refused word processing training by her manager, who felt that her disability would inevitably limit the work she could undertake. She therefore attended evening classes to acquire this skill. However, the only word-processing equipment has to be

shared by all members of the workgroup, so she is unable to practise regularly enough to become proficient. Joyce has also said she would like to acquire computing skills, but again the manager has not been encouraging. She feels that lack of these skills will impede her progress: *'I know I will be looking for a change of work in a year or so. Maybe I'll ask to be moved to Accounts. I would like more responsibility. If it was a more interesting job I wouldn't want to change so regularly. I do my interesting things out of work, and when I come to work I really switch my mind off because the work is so mundane. They say I can't be a supervisor because I can't use the telephone, but there are no aids here which might help me. I've always been a leader. I am Chairman of a club for deaf people and I teach sign language to hearing people. I know that if I was hearing I would definitely like to be a supervisor or a manager.'*

(b) People with disabilities may well be carrying out less visible tasks which are frequently overlooked when assessing performance but which are none the less essential. People tend to identify tasks someone is *not* doing rather than take account of those they are doing.

(c) It is important for staff with disabilities to be given as wide a range of tasks and jobs as practical even if their existing skills and expertise appear to lie in one direction, and appear limited or non-existent in others. Such impressions may be based on unfounded assumptions about an individual's abilities and aspirations and on their opportunities being restricted in the past.

The example in (a) above illustrates both of these issues

(d) People with disabilities may want to develop their careers but may not talk of this for a variety of reasons: they may lack confidence; they may fear possible negative consequences if they ask for a change; they may know little of other jobs and vacancies in the organisation; they may not want to be a 'bother'; they may fear that the extra support they might need on occasions may not be available in a different job.

Barbara, a clerical officer with a kidney condition and high blood pressure, is felt by her manager to have management potential. Because of her medical condition the company doctor has recommended she be transferred to a less stressful area of work. Her manager, aware of her condition, has suggested she apply for promotion as well as transfer, but the clerical officer is reluctant to do so. The manager acknowledges that *'someone who is moved on health grounds may be held back in the promotion stakes. I cannot guarantee that it will not happen, although I hope it doesn't. She has got excellent skills and the ability to rise, and will make an excellent manager, so I hope it will not hold her back in the long term. Her problem may only be a temporary one anyway.'*

(e) A manager and/or supervisor may well need to be proactive about the career development of a person with a disability for a variety of reasons: their work experience may not have followed a standard or usual pattern; they may lack a breadth of experience whilst having specialist knowledge and skills; they may, through restricted mobility or communication skills, lack the 'grapevine' knowledge others in the organisation are assumed to have of jobs and vacancies; they may fear problems or barriers which do not exist or which can be easily overcome; they may assume their disability stops them from being considered for promotion.

The manager of George, who has diabetes, has been instrumental in helping him to progress from storekeeper to management trainee in the Personnel function. THIS HAS BEEN ACHIEVED BY ENCOURAGING INTERNAL TRANSFER, BY RECOMMENDING GEORGE FOR TRAINING IN A WIDE RANGE OF SUBJECTS, AND BY FACILITATING PERSONAL DEVELOPMENT THROUGH GRADUALLY INCREASING LEVELS OF RESPONSIBILITY. George injects himself with insulin twice a day, preferably at home before and after work, and tries to ensure regular meal-times. If he stays late at work to attend a meeting, his manager arranges transport home *'rather than chance his bus breaking down'*. This is the only special arrangement made because of the disability.

The supervisor of Robert, a computer programmer who has muscular dystrophy, says of his colleague: *'There should be no problems if he wanted to move into management, but he has never said he wants to. He would need to attend more meetings and give presentations. Sometimes he gives the impression that he has resigned himself to his lot.'* Robert himself would very much like to progress, but sees little likelihood of promotion into management: *'At that level you've got to fit into the management structure, you've got to play golf and have the right handshake. I don't know anyone disabled who is in management.'*

SMALL CAPITALS DENOTE GOOD PRACTICE

Knowledge, Information and Skill Needs

Managers and others responsible for career development need to know:

Knowledge and Information

1. What jobs and vacancies exist in the organisation and what skills and experience they require.

2. Ways to develop the expertise of a person with a disability who may possibly have had a restricted range of experience.

3. Whether a person with a disability is willing and able to undertake additional duties which may take them out of the workplace. If so, whether any special provisions need to be made.

4. What training exists, internally and externally, (including from specialist disability organisations) to enable individuals to equip themselves for alternative work.

Skills

1. How to appraise an individual's performance taking into account all aspects of the work they undertake.

2. How to establish, if someone is not doing a 'standard' job, whether the range of tasks they do and the level of performance they reach is within acceptable limits.

3. How to judge an individual's ability to carry out or train for other tasks and jobs.

4. How to ascertain from the individual what their aspirations are and how these might be achieved, even if the individual may be reticent about stating ambitions.

5. How to intercede if the career development of a person with a disability is being impeded unjustifiably by the negative attitudes of others.

6. How to counsel an individual if their ambition and aspirations are unrealistic in relation to available opportunities within the organisation.

7. How to ensure that others who are able to influence an individual's career development are fully appraised of the person's achievements and aspirations.

11. Promotion and Transfer

Key Issues

(a) A person with a disability may need detailed information about other jobs available and the working environment (e.g. where they are located) before deciding whether to apply.

> Several people with disabilities expressed reservations about applying for other jobs, whether inside or outside their organisations, even though they felt their abilities were underused. They feared losing the security they had and they also feared rejection by new colleagues. They also expressed concern that they might cause problems for others if the new work place, or manager or job, made demands on them they were unable to meet. Having detailed information about other jobs available and the working environment, would help overcome some of these reservations, as they could make a realistic assessment of their ability to do the jobs before applying.

(b) Promotion and transfer arrangements may unwittingly militate against people with disabilities (e.g. the location, height and print of internal advertisements; information about vacancies being obtained mainly through an informal network).

> Internal vacancies in one large organisation are advertised on a display board. As it is not located in a main thoroughfare, anyone interested in a vacancy has to visit that part of the building especially to see the board. However, most employees get information about internal vacancies by informal means, often by chatting to colleagues in other departments. This is less easy for a person with a hearing disability. The supervisor of one such person said: *'People can only progress here by getting transfers. I hope that Tim reads the board to keep in touch with vacancies.'*

(c) Senior staff who are influential in making promotion decisions may not be sufficiently aware of an individual's achievements and aspirations. The supervisor or line manager of a person with a disability may need actively to make such facts more widely known.

> In general, senior managers were aware of those parts of a job a person with a disability was *not* doing. Supervisors and line managers knew of the additional tasks the person undertook or the specialist role they had developed. They were also more aware of the individual's achievements outside work and of their aspirations.

(d) An apparent lack of interest in promotion on the part of a person with a disability may be due to a temporary health problem, or it may conceal a very real interest tempered with apprehension (e.g. about acceptance by new colleagues or by existing colleagues of a new status; about managing a disability in an unknown environment).

> A man with a heart condition and a woman with high blood pressure were each thought by their managers to have management potential. They both refused to apply for promotion. Although neither mentioned it to their manager, they both intended to reconsider this decision when their medical condition stabilised.

Knowledge, Information and Skill Needs

Managers and others with responsibilities relating to promotion and transfer need to know:

Knowledge and Information

1. The abilities and aspirations of members of staff with disabilities in order to find out what jobs in the organisation might be suitable for them and what training might equip them for such jobs.

2. The requirements and components of jobs in the organisation in sufficient detail to help an individual decide whether they would wish and be able to undertake them (with aids and adaptations if necessary).

3. Any difficulties members of staff have with promotion and transfer arrangements in the organisation, and who to contact about making possible changes to these.

4. Expressed or perceived lack of interest in promotion may be transient and does not necessarily mean that the individual will never wish to take on additional responsibilities.

5. The responsibility of the supervisor or line manager of a person with a disability includes the need to make known to senior staff that individual's achievements and aspirations.

Skills

1. How to ascertain the abilities and skills of a staff member, including those acquired away from paid work which may not always be recognised by them as relevant to the work situation.

2. How to analyse components of jobs and obtain information about the working environment which may be important to an individual with a disability.

3. How to match the demands of a job to an individual's ability and potential to do the job, with aids, adaptations or other assistance if appropriate.

4. How to help an individual decide whether they would be interested in, and could realistically undertake, a new job, such advice being based upon knowledge of the individual's ability and potential and the requirements of the job rather than assumptions about limitations imposed by a disability.

5. How to persuade others to give an individual the opportunity to undertake additional or different work.

12. Dealing with Organisational and Work Changes

Key Issues

(a) Any change in existing working arrangements, even if slight, may have more implications for employees with disabilities and their immediate work colleagues than for other employees, e.g. a change of location; staff, supervisory or management changes; new tasks, technology, products; change in hours of work or staff numbers.

> One organisation arranged, as part of its safety procedure, that staff with sensory disabilities should not work alone. This arrangement became inoperable when flexitime was introduced.

SMALL CAPITALS DENOTE GOOD PRACTICE

A person who uses a wheelchair and her colleagues decided to rearrange their office. The supervisor said: 'WE REORGANISED OUR DESKS RECENTLY, SIMPLY BECAUSE WE ALL FANCIED A CHANGE. OUR FIRST THOUGHT WAS 'WILL THE WHEELCHAIR GO THROUGH THAT SPACE?' IT WASN'T A PROBLEM, BUT IT WAS IMPORTANT TO THINK ABOUT IT.'

(b) Consulting staff with disabilities before finalising plans can avoid causing otherwise unforeseen difficulties for them and others. People with disabilities are very aware of the implications for them of change, and can often make practical recommendations which will be of help to all staff.

WHEN CONSIDERING THE ARCHITECTS' PLANS FOR A NEW BUILDING, SENIOR MANAGERS INVITED TWO MEMBERS OF STAFF WHO USE WHEEL-CHAIRS TO A MEETING TO DISCUSS PROVISION IN THE NEW PREMISES FOR PEOPLE WITH DISABILITIES. One suggestion they made was for a covered way to be erected between the car park and the main entrance, a distance of about a hundred yards. This is being considered as it will benefit all staff as well as visitors in wet weather. Although they appreciated the opportunity to make a contribution to the discussions, the two individuals selected felt unqualified to represent all staff with disabilities: *'We had to try to think of the needs of people with other kinds of disabilities, people with poor eyesight who would need special lighting and signs, and people with other kinds of concerns.'*

(c) At times of change rumours abound, and staff with disabilities will have fears even if not expressed. It may be possible to allay these by providing factual information as early as possible, and discussing aspects causing concern.

An impressive large building is being constructed adjacent to the more traditional office premises it is shortly to replace. Douglas knows he will be transferring to the new block when it has been completed, and has been informed that planning has included the provision of ramps at the main entrance to ensure wheelchair access. He has also been promised a reserved parking bay within a hundred yards of that entrance. However Douglas still has many concerns about his future working environment which have not been discussed, and these continue to cause anxiety. When modernisation of the existing building took place some time ago, people using manual wheelchairs found it increasingly difficult to move around the working areas: *'Carpets and swing doors, particularly heavy fire doors, are the scourge of this place'*. Douglas fears that similar obstacles may restrict his movement within the new premises. He has not been told which floor he will be working on, but he has heard rumours that the new working areas will be open plan and that meetings rooms will be located away from these. As his work requires him to visit other departments he is anxious as to whether all working areas, as well as the meetings rooms and public areas, will be fully accessible. A colleague commented: *'I often see Douglas sitting in his chair looking anxiously out of the window at the building works. He is often there watching them. He is probably wondering if he is going to be able to manage in the new building.'*

(d) Special training is available for people with disabilities in a wide variety of skills and subject matter. Much of this provision has been designed to equip people with the skills needed in a changing work environment.

> ONE PERSON HAD ATTENDED IN THE EVENINGS A NUMBER OF SPECIAL TRAINING COURSES FOR PEOPLE WITH HEARING DISABILITIES TO FAMILIARISE THEM WITH NEW OFFICE TECHNOLOGY. She was, however, the only person interviewed who had taken advantage of such training facilities.

Knowledge, Information and Skill Needs

Managers and others planning and implementing organisational and work changes need to know:

Knowledge and Information

1. Any possible changes in the organisation as far ahead as possible in order to be able to plan for and minimise possible negative consequences for staff.

2. Who to contact about meeting any special needs of staff with disabilities.

3. What training exists internally and externally for people with disabilities which might equip them for work changes.

Skills

1. How to find out from an employee with a disability whether they have special needs which should be considered when planning for change.

2. How to provide information about planned changes and discuss staff fears about the implications of such changes.

3. How to involve a staff member with a disability in planning for change without causing them additional concern or embarrassment.

4. How to monitor the effects of change for staff with special needs, and help them to overcome any difficulties created.

5. How to find out at an early stage what the implications of any changes may be for staff with disabilities, and how to minimise any possible adverse effects.

6. How to monitor the effects for staff with disabilities of organisational or work changes once they have been implemented.

13. Relations with Customers

Key Issues

(a) Aspects of the working environment which create difficulties for employees with disabilities are likely also to be problematic for existing or potential customers.

Glass partitions between cashiers and customers in many banks and building societies can present difficulties of communication to both. People who work in a branch which employs a member of staff with a disability are particularly aware of difficulties experienced by customers: 'WE OFTEN GO OUT FRONT AND SIT AND TALK DIRECTLY WITH AN ELDERLY PERSON OR CUSTOMERS WITH SIGHT OR HEARING DISABILITIES. *People who are below average height or in wheelchairs can't see over the counter, and can't reach up to write. The cash dispenser outside is also difficult because of the combination of height and angle. When the sun is shining on the screen it's hard for everyone to see it. It's impossible for anyone in a wheelchair.'*

An organisation which provides services to the public has one location which presents considerable difficulties to the many people who visit, as well as staff both with and without disabilities. The large building is not located near public transport, nor does it offer any parking provision. Both the main and side entrances are reached by long flights of steps. The offices are located on the upper floors of the building, which is shared with a number of other organisations. There is no receptionist on the ground floor to direct visitors. An information board is located near the lifts, giving the floor numbers for each organisation but not indicating which offices or departments are on each floor. The two lifts each stop on alternate floors only. A manager commented: *'Members of the public have to be able to come here, but we know there are problems of access for those who are partially sighted or using wheelchairs. One or two people have not been able to get here and we have heard about them and visited them at home, but there may well be others who do not come because they are not able to.'*

(b) If the needs of people with disabilities are taken into account at the planning stage (e.g. when designing new services) better facilities are likely to result for everyone.

ONE ORGANISATION, WHOSE PREMISES ARE REGULARLY VISITED BY MEMBERS OF THE PUBLIC, IS PARTICULARLY CONSCIOUS OF THE GOOD- WILL GENERATED BY ITS CAREFUL PLANNING POLICY: *'We have always had a policy in our organisation to make our entrances a ramp rather than steps. We have benefited in general from that. It means that people with pushchairs or shopping trolleys and the elderly, as well as those using wheelchairs, are more easily able to get into our offices.'*

(c) Senior management fears of negative customer reactions to employees with visible disabilities are rarely shared by those with direct customer involvement, and are hardly ever justified. The image of the organisation is generally enhanced when people with disabilities are seen to be employed.

A cashier with a visual disability has to hold documents very close in order to read them. Spectacles do not aid her vision, but because customers frequently suggested she should be wearing them she now wears pale sun-glasses at work. These have benefited her by reducing the glare of bright lights. Her supervisor suggested that customers comment because the disability is not obvious: *'A lot of people don't think of her as disabled because she doesn't look it. It's when she has her nose close up against the screen that customers say "Can she see?" They probably think "what's she doing on the till?"'* Once a relationship is established, however, customer reactions are much more positive, largely because *'she is good at talking to people, both face to face and on the telephone.'*

When a person who uses a wheelchair was recruited to a front-line job involving a great deal of customer contact, the line manager expressed reservations: *'We were concerned about possible prejudice from our customers. But everyone has a nice word to say for him. A number of customers regularly ask for "the chap with the wheelchair".'*

Knowledge, Information and Skill Needs

Managers and others seeking to enhance customer relations need to know:

Knowledge and Information needed

1. Which aspects of the working environment present difficulties to people with disabilities, whether employees, customers, potential customers or visitors, and what guidance and help is available both internally and externally to improve these.

2. The importance of advising all staff how to deal with customer criticism, and where a member of staff directly involved has a disability, of not internalising such criticism or assuming it is disability-related.

Skills

1. How to involve people with disabilities in the design of customer services.

2. How to make senior management aware of 'front line' jobs successfully being done by staff with visible disabilities, and the resultant benefit to customer relations.

3. How to advise a staff member with a disability on ways of dealing with criticism or negative reactions from a customer.

4. How to discuss and agree with a staff member with a disability and their colleagues ways of explaining unusual behaviour to a customer, should this be necessary.

5. How to involve staff with disabilities when planning customer services, so that more special needs of customers and potential customers are met.

14. Implementing the Organisation's Disability Policy

Key Issues

(a) All line and personnel managers and supervisors need to understand what the philosophy, objectives and implications are of their organisation's policy on the employment of people with disabilities.

ONE ORGANISATION PROJECTS A POSITIVE IMAGE OF ENCOURAGING THE EMPLOYMENT OF PEOPLE WITH DISABILITIES IN THE POLICY STATEMENT INCLUDED IN THEIR ANNUAL REPORT. But several people thought there was an informal unwritten policy of limiting the numbers of people with disabilities in order to successfully employ a few.

Most people interviewed did not know whether their organisation had a policy on the employment of people with disabilities, or what it contained. Where a policy was known about, most individuals did not know how it should be interpreted or implemented.

(b) Once the decision has been taken that the organisation should develop an active and positive policy towards the employment of people with disabilities, managers and supervisors will need guidance and information on how to implement it.

ONE MANAGER HAD RECEIVED INFORMATION ON IMPLEMENTING HIS ORGANISATION'S SPECIAL SCHEME FOR RECRUITING MORE PEOPLE WITH DISABILITIES, but he did not know how the policy required him to deal with increased sickness or a deteriorating medical condition. He expressed the need for guidance if either of these eventualities arose in relation to either a new or existing member of staff.

(c) Consulting people with disabilities, both employees and others, on how best to implement the essential elements of such a policy will help to avoid inappropriate and ineffective action.

ONE ORGANISATION HAS PRODUCED A RESOURCE PACK ON DISABILITIES. IT IS DESIGNED BOTH FOR MANAGERS *'TO MAKE THEM AWARE OF THEIR RESPONSIBILITIES'* AND FOR EMPLOYEES WITH DISABILITIES *'TO LET THEM KNOW WHAT IS AVAILABLE'.* IT IS BEING SENT IN DRAFT FORM TO A NUMBER OF PEOPLE WITH DISABILITIES AT DIFFERENT LEVELS IN THE ORGANISATION FOR THEIR COMMENTS AND SUGGESTIONS BEFORE BEING PRINTED AND CIRCULATED.

(d) Any policy should be monitored to ensure its effectiveness, and the results should be publicised so that people both internally and externally, including potential recruits, know that the policy exists and what its aims and achievements are.

ONE ORGANISATION HAS STARTED TO MONITOR THE EFFECTIVENESS OF ITS POLICY IN TERMS OF THE NUMBERS OF PEOPLE WITH DISABILITIES RECRUITED AND RETAINED, but not as yet their progression although this is planned. IT IS ALSO PRODUCING GUIDELINES FOR ALL LEVELS OF STAFF ON HOW ITS POLICY SHOULD BE IMPLEMENTED, AND A LEAFLET FOR POTENTIAL RECRUITS TELLING THEM ABOUT THE POLICY AND ITS ACHIEVEMENTS TO DATE.

Knowledge, Information and Skill Needs

Managers and others responsible for implementing the organisation's disability policy need to know:

Knowledge and Information

1. What the policy is, and the practical implications for them of meeting its objectives.

2. Their own role and the roles of others in the organisation in implementing the policy.

3. Who in the organisation can provide information and guidance on action to be taken.

4. What advice and information staff should receive on the policy in order to maximise its effectiveness.

5. What assistance, equipment, information, training and advice exists both internally and externally for a staff member with a disability, their manager, supervisor and colleagues.

6. Who in the organisation is responsible for making contact with statutory, professional and voluntary sources of assistance.

Skills

1. How to ensure all staff are fully informed of, and actively involved in, implementing the organisation's policy on the employment of people with disabilities.

2. How to monitor the effectiveness of the policy as it relates to members of staff managed or supervised.

3. How to publicise the aims and achievements of the policy both internally and externally.

Chapter 3

Priorities in Meeting Training Needs

Who needs Training?

We have talked as though the needs for information, skills and training of managers and supervisors were synonymous, but this is not of course so. The titles 'manager' and 'supervisor' each cover an immense range of responsibilities and levels of authority. Some of the 'supervisors' of the people with disabilities who we interviewed were in fact managers.

From the point of view of disability management, and the training needs related to it, we have identified four key groups of people, but they are by no means the only people with training needs. Each individual has the potential to become disabled. Everyone in employment may at some stage work with, or make decisions which affect, a colleague with a disability. Training about disability management is therefore relevant, or potentially relevant, to everyone. Because universal training on disability issues is currently unlikely in most organisations, we have concentrated on those who are most directly involved on an ongoing basis. These are:

- people who themselves have a disability

- the person, whether manager or supervisor, who is the immediate superior of the person with the disability, in day-to-day working contact with them

- the people, usually managers, higher in the hierarchy who are involved in making decisions about staff but are not in hour-to-hour or day-to-day contact with their work

- the people in staff jobs who advise line managers and who, because of their specialist role, influence staffing decisions e.g. personnel, welfare, medical, premises, equal opportunities staff.

The last three groups may, of course, include people who themselves have a disability.

People with Disabilities

It is often assumed that the person with a disability will make known any difficulty experienced at work if they find it necessary, and will ask for help when appropriate. It is also often assumed that they will have access to, or know about, sources of advice and assistance. If the supervisor has a key role as a 'communicator' (see below), the person with a disability has a key role as an 'information provider', and this may extend to general disability issues rather than only those associated with their own disability. To perform this role people with disabilities need to know about:

· their own disability and any work implications

· wider disability management issues

· job requirements

· sources of information, advice, equipment (and funding where appropriate) both within the organisation and externally.

They also need the skill and confidence both to articulate such information and to assist their career development generally.

Immediate Supervisors

The needs of this group in relation to disability management are very much to do with day-to-day management issues:

· the best way to organise on-the-job training

· how to judge an individual's performance and help improve it if it is not adequate

· how to maintain overall production when an individual employee's productivity varies through absence, personal or health difficulties

· how to build and keep a strong team.

They also have to communicate both formally and informally with their manager as to the strengths and weaknesses in their team, and ensure people's achievements are known, as well as any difficulties. This role of the supervisor as communicator has emerged as a key one in relation to employees with disabilities. The supervisor plays a key role in dispelling misconceptions and avoiding stereotypes amongst others, crucially amongst more senior management.

More Senior Managers

This group, the more senior managers, who do not directly supervise the person with a disability, have somewhat different needs.

They may well know little of the actual work content and standards of performance of an employee. In the absence of these they may resort to stereotypes, and make incorrect assumptions. They may perceive problems in relation to disability of which others more immediately involved are unaware. In so doing they sometimes overlook a disabled individual's achievements and underestimate their potential.

They need to know an individual's strengths and their true worth to the work group. They also need to know of any problems the individual may need help to overcome. This is because they may well take the final decisions on probation, appraisal reports, attendance on training courses, promotion and redeployment, and pay, or make recommendations to their own manager on these.

They may be the main point of contact with people outside their function, for example with personnel, and through them with external disability agencies which provide assistance. Their need is to know who, within and outside the organisation, they can contact for help.

In addition, if they are involved in recruitment and selection decisions they need to know how to arrange and carry out these procedures in such a way as not to exclude likely recruits.

It is also important that senior managers responsible for policy development understand the implications of their decisions as they affect those more closely involved with disability management.

Specialist Advisors

This group - the specialist advisors - have needs not dissimilar to those of managers. But because they are dealing with many different managers and staff members, and work situations, they need more in-depth skills and knowledge. The research did not address directly the needs of these people, but their role in disability management has emerged as crucial. Whether or not they are formally designated as responsible for disability issues, they need to understand the significance for people with disabilities of personnel and other organisational policies and practices, and to be able to advise on the possible consequences. They also need to be aware of internal and external sources of help. Specialist advisors may be in the personnel function, but staff in other departments, such as occupational health, welfare and premises, may have a role of this kind.

Other Groups

In addition to the four key groups, there are others with specific training needs relating to disability management. Another way of deciding where training needs exist is to look at the functions performed by people. Such analysis reveals the following, sometimes overlapping, groups:

- *all those involved in recruitment and selection,* including receptionists, gatekeepers and clerical staff in personnel departments. Line or personnel managers, who draw up job descriptions, place advertisements, sift applications, interview, test and select candidates, need to know how to avoid unwittingly discouraging or rejecting suitable candidates who happen to have a disability. Medical staff, who may advise managers on the work implications of a particular person's disability, also need to know in detail what the job in question consists of in order to give informed advice.

- *personnel and line managers and supervisors involved in the induction of new staff* need to ensure that they meet the needs of new recruits with disabilities, for example if attention needs to be paid to issues of access to buildings or if extra information should be given to the new recruit.

- *staff responsible for the design, refurbishment and maintenance of buildings and equipment* need particular knowledge. Installing a special 'disabled toilet' may be a grand, expensive and wasted gesture if it can only be reached by stairs with no handrail, or if the door handles are too high for someone in a wheelchair to reach.

- *training staff,* whether employed by the organisation or external consultants, need to consider issues of access to premises and to training materials. They need to know how to ensure that information is presented to participants on courses in ways which minimise problems for people with visual or hearing disabilities. If they are to be involved in disability training, they themselves will first need in-depth training on wider aspects of disability in order to be able to develop and handle material sensitively and confidently.

- *trade union and employee representatives, and health and safety representatives* need to know how to avert and deal with disability-related problems.

- *occupational health staff* may be assumed by virtue of their training to be able to advise on all issues, but they may lack detailed knowledge of the individual and/or the work situation.

- *the colleagues of a person with a disability* may well feel that they lack the necessary skills and knowledge to interact sensitively and confidently with a disabled colleague.

- *personnel and welfare staff*, particularly those with formal responsibility for disability issues, need in-depth skills and knowledge in order to be able to give managers and staff both information and advice.

- finally, and arguably most importantly, *senior managers*, who have to formulate or agree a policy on disability management, need an understanding of issues if they are to be able to make informed judgements.

How to Provide Training

Ideally training on disability issues should become an integrated part of all management and supervisory training. But this presupposes conditions which do not exist in any of the organisations researched:

- that all managers and supervisors attend regular updating in-house management training courses.

- that disability is seen as a high-priority issue for which time on existing courses must be found. Equal opportunity issues relating to gender, race and disability are seen as an important component of management training in only one of the three organisations in which we carried out research. Even in this organisation many managers and supervisors have not had any disability-related training.

- that trainers have sufficient knowledge and in-depth understanding of disability issues to be able to develop and present material confidently and sensitively. Distance learning can have an important place in providing factual information. But the situations which managers and supervisors deal with in relation to disability, also require them to have quite refined inter-personal and analytical skills. With regard to interviewing, for example, the research shows a lack of confidence on the part of managers and supervisors to talk

95

directly to a person with a disability about any practical consequences of this disability. They may also need help in learning to deal with the possibly negative reaction of colleagues or customers. This kind of experience is best gained in an interactive learning situation where they can learn to phrase questions, or give information, get feedback and gauge people's reactions.

Training will undoubtedly benefit from the presence in the tutor group of people with disabilities. However, asking one individual, who is inexperienced in training, to join a course as the 'expert' because they have personal experience of one kind of disability can be both counterproductive and extremely stressful for the individual concerned. There are now a number of experienced and skilled trainers who have disabilities, who could present or co-tutor courses.

Chapter 4

Organisational Issues

People's Understanding of Disability

Different interpretations of the word 'disability', and its relationship with handicap, result in the differences of approach which organisations follow when recruiting and employing people with disabilities.

The *Employer's Guide to Disabilities* (Kettle and Massie, 1986) makes the following distinction between disability and handicap:

> 'Put simply, "disability" is the total or partial loss of a functional ability. A person who has lost an eye has the partial loss of the functional ability to see - the person has a disability. Alternatively, a "handicap" is the disadvantage arising from the disability . . . Whether a disability gives rise to a handicap or not will largely depend on the environment in which the individual finds himself.'

In each of the three organisations researched (see Appendix 5 for organisational profiles) the relationship between disability and handicap is interpreted differently, with the result that approaches to disability management also vary considerably. For example:

- in Organisation A the assumption is made that a disability will result in the individual being handicapped at work, but that the handicap can be overcome with help. People with disabilities are recruited under a special scheme on the basis that they are not expected to achieve the same level of performance as others in the same time, but will do so eventually. Additional learning time is made available, and any special equipment or modifications provided, but other resources, for example extra training, have not been thought necessary by managers even if requested by individuals or their supervisors. Disability issues are looked after by local managers, with the support of a central welfare department.

- in Organisation B disability is equated with handicap. Only a small proportion of the staff are known to have disabilities. These include a few individuals who are substantially dependent upon the help

Problem

of colleagues and other staff. Some managers are consequently reluctant to accept people with disabilities in their department, seeing them as a liability *'needing extra consideration'* rather than an asset. Where people with disabilities have been recruited, they are sometimes regarded by senior staff as *'unable to do a whole job'* and assumed not to have the potential to progress, even though their line managers have reported on their valuable, sometimes special- ist, role. Medical staff are responsible for disability, as well as health, concerns, but one nurse interviewed said that if a problem was brought to her which she did not think resulted from a health problem, she *'would not touch it.'* In consequence, a person with a hearing disability did not know who to ask about the possibility of fitting a visual alarm linked to the fire bell.

· in Organisation C the approach is taken that much of the handicap associated with disability in fact results from an inadequate work- ing environment, for example inappropriate job placement or people's negative attitudes. Disability is regarded primarily as an equal opportunity issue. The small team responsible for disability issues concentrates mainly on policy development and monitoring. As a result individuals with disabilities sometimes feel that their personal needs are being overlooked, and they do not know who to turn to for practical advice or information.

Individuals, as well as organisations, interpret disability in different ways. Some of those interviewed felt that their organisations linked disability with *'being registered disabled'*. Others had different perceptions of what constitutes a disability, for example multiple sclerosis, diabetes and epilepsy were all described as *'not really disabilities'*. Individuals found particular difficulty in dealing with 'invisible' disabilities, such as deafness.

It was also perhaps significant that all four people who revealed a disability when interviewed, but had not made it known to their organisa- tions, were in management positions in two of the organisations. Although they managed their disabilities unaided, each described situations at work which they found difficult and where some assistance could be helpful. Although not directly stated, it is possible that they refrained from officially seeking assistance because they feared this might prejudice their status or promotion prospects.

Whose Responsibility is the Management of Disability at Work?

The research has mainly concentrated on the needs of line managers and supervisors at work, but responsibility does not start and end with them.

The person with the major responsibility for the management of disability is of course the individual with the disability. It is they who know how to avoid and minimise most problems connected with their disability. For instance, someone with a bad back will try to ensure that as far as possible he or she does nothing at work which will bring about a disabling attack. Provided their job allows such flexibility the bad back will seldom, if ever, be a handicap at work. Most organisations recognise and accept that the prime responsibility lies with the individual and base any disability policy, formal or informal, on this.

It was pointed out that to some extent the seniority of the person with a disability will determine the extent to which they manage their own disability. For example, a manager with diabetes who needs to eat at regular intervals can often arrange meetings to fit in with this requirement. A less senior member of staff works in a more closely controlled environment and may not have this flexibility.

In the case of people whose disabilities do or could handicap them at work, there may be occasions when others within the organisation will be involved in management of the disability. The person with a bad back may, for example, only be able to perform a sedentary job if a special chair is provided. Colleagues may be asked to help with lifting or reaching. If the individual is not fully mobile, the Safety Officer may recommend a special evacuation procedure. All of these people need some skills and knowledge if they are to operate confidently and competently.

Disability-related skills and knowledge can be needed at any stage in an individual's working life, but particularly when circumstances change, for example when new products or services are introduced, when a new work-group is formed, or when jobs are relocated.

The Role of Medical Staff in the Management of Disability

There is a technical aspect relating to disability management which is absent from other aspects of equal opportunity management. The role of the medical profession, (in the shape of occupational health nurses employed by organisations, GPs and specialists retained by organisations on a part-time basis, or full-time occupational health specialists) is different in each organisation. These differences show some of the important, and sometimes controversial, issues surrounding medical staff and their role in disability management.

Medical practitioners are involved, in all three organisations, in the decision as to whether someone with a 'health' problem should be recruited, and often disability is wrongly equated with ill-health. The advice of the medical practitioners can be given without much knowledge of the actual components of the job for which the person is being considered. Because the advice is being given by a professional to personnel or line managers who usually lack medical knowledge or knowledge of disabilities, the advice will usually be accepted.

The research points to the need for steps to be taken to develop more systematic matching of people with jobs than currently exists in most organisations. It seems inevitable that, given most personnel and line managers' current limited knowledge of disability issues, and the medical profession's limited knowledge of job requirements, people who could be useful employees are being excluded from jobs they could, in fact, perform satisfactorily.

Another related issue is that of who should know the details of an individual's disability, and how and when they should be told. In the researched organisations it is not common practice for the medical practitioners, or occupational health staff who hold the confidential medical information on an individual, to pass down information to personnel and line managers or consult the individual about the possibility of doing so. As managers do not on the whole ask the individual about the practical consequences of their disability, their decisions are often based on incorrect assumptions.

Communicating about Disability Issues

The importance of more open discussion about disability issues was recognised by people at all levels in all three organisations. Managers and supervisors need accurate information in order to make informed decisions and take appropriate action. People with disabilities often have the most relevant information, and in turn they need the opportunity to express their own preferences and requirements. Asking for help can be as difficult, or more so, than offering help.

In spite of the need and desire to communicate about disability issues, however, almost everyone interviewed expressed reservations about their ability to do so effectively. People without disabilities said they were 'afraid to hurt anyone's feelings', while those they were anxious not to offend were 'not wanting to draw attention' or 'afraid of being a nuisance.'

A number of people were unsure whether they should be asking for information about an individual's disability, either from the person concerned or indirectly, because *'all medical information is confidential - only the medical staff have access to it.'*

An additional barrier to communicating openly about disability issues was the lack of a formal procedure or specific opportunity to do so. For example, people were unsure whether to raise the topic at a selection interview, during induction, once they had established close working relationships, or only if and when necessary. The work implications of more obvious disabilities - for example, access to the workplace for someone using a wheelchair - were more likely to be discussed at an early stage. However, disability-related issues were often only discussed because a difficulty had arisen. This applied particularly where people with 'invisible' disabilities were concerned.

Organisations need to consider ways to facilitate the exchange of disability-related information both between individuals and at a corporate level. For example, the existence of the special Disability Support Unit in Organisation C was unknown by some of that organisation's employees, while others did not know its role or function. In Organisation B no one directly involved knew who should be responsible for arranging to fit a visual fire alarm for the benefit of people with hearing disabilities. When a problem arose in Organisation A relating to a person with a visual disability, there was uncertainty about who should seek outside advice or from where. In both latter organisations, the individuals most closely concerned - those with the disability and their immediate supervisors - had accurately identified the problem and its causes and could suggest how it might be overcome. However, there was no clear line of upward communication which would result in action being taken.

One situation in which the ability of a colleague, supervisor or manager to communicate effectively about a disability may be crucial, is if they are asked by the individual with the disability to act as their representative, take action on their behalf, or help present their point of view. An example might be a disciplinary hearing where the individual concerned has a disability which restricts their ability to communicate (e.g. speech or hearing). Other situations arise which also require knowledgeable intervention. For example, a blind applicant for promotion filled in the relevant form when at home ill and had no one to check it. He would have liked his manager to have done so, but because they did not discuss disability issues the manager did not recognise this need.

How can Communication be Improved?

The few individuals interviewed who had received some training which touched upon disability issues had all found that this gave them the confidence to open up the subject themselves. For example, interviewing skills training which included discussion about interviewing people with disabilities had helped one person ask appropriate questions in an inoffensive way to get the information needed. Some people with disabilities had developed the confidence to articulate their own needs by attending assertiveness training.

Where discussion of disability issues is built into the recruitment procedure, for example during induction, people can gain the confidence of knowing both that they *should* be raising such issues, and that this is the appropriate time for them to do so. Responsibilities can also be clearly defined.

At a more informal level, people can discuss disability in a more relaxed and confident way if disability is regarded and treated throughout the organisation as part of a continuum, with 'complete ability' at one end of the scale and 'complete inability' at the other. No one would regard themselves as being at either extreme, with the implication that everyone is more or less 'able' depending on the characteristics being measured.

The Role of Policy in the Management of Disability at Work

The research was carried out in three organisations with very different approaches to issues affecting the management of disability at work, and therefore three very different policies (see Appendix 5 for profiles of the organisations).

Organisation A, developed a unique policy two years ago. This aimed at increasing the recruitment of people with disabilities, by providing managers with an incentive to do so. Thirty-two supernumerary posts were created. Regional managers select locations into which a person with a disability will be recruited as a supernumerary member of staff. It is possible for someone who reaches standard performance levels to be taken onto the staff establishment if a vacancy arises and for another supernumerary recruit therefore to replace them.

Organisation B is like the majority of medium-sized and large organisations in this country. It complies with the Companies Regulations in stating publicly its policy in relation to employees with disabilities in its annual report.

The formal responsibility for this policy seems to fall on the shoulders of the senior personnel manager, who is responsible for equal opportunity issues and within whose department the list of registered disabled people is kept. However, as the organisation is decentralised, any day-to-day issues or problems are dealt with locally by line and personnel managers and their staff, possibly involving occupational health staff.

The organisation has taken no steps as yet to implement its stated policy, and several members of staff believe that the informal policy of the organisation is to limit the numbers of employees with disabilities. This is said to be in order to ensure that those in the organisation are able to deal positively with employees who do have disabilities.

The organisation's approach could be said to be ad hoc, leaving disability management very much to individual expertise and goodwill. This has resulted in a small number of people with disabilities being recruited, and staff who become disabled being treated with consideration. The policy seems to work well when the person with the disability is articulate, confident, pleasant and sufficiently assertive to be able to make their needs clear in a way to which other staff react positively.

Such an ad hoc approach, however, can have disadvantages. A disabled employee had to be lifted from his car to a wheelchair and back at the beginning and end of each day. This was left to volunteers in his department who were not given training in lifting. One injured his back as a result.

Organisation C is very unusual in having developed a comprehensive equal opportunity policy backed up with central and departmental resources and training. Within an equal opportunity unit in the Personnel department, three staff have specific responsibility for developing and monitoring policies in relation to disability. Procedure guidelines have been produced relating to the employment of people with disabilities.

Training has been provided both for staff with disabilities and for other managers and supervisors. The former has included a clerical and office skills course for people with hearing disabilities, and a career development course and information seminar for staff with disabilities. Training for managers and supervisors has included:

- equal opportunity and disability issues being covered in selection interviewing courses

- a course on disability and employment for managers who work with people with disabilities, and for personnel staff and anyone in an advisory role for people with disabilities

- a deaf awareness course for managers and colleagues of those who are known to have hearing disabilities.

The three organisations also illustrate three different approaches to the development of a disability policy and its resourcing. In Organisation A the welfare officer and her assistant have disability issues as an important part of their role. In Organisation B a senior personnel manager, who has equal opportunity as one of his many responsibilities, is regarded as the person responsible for issues relating to disability. In Organisation C an equal opportunity unit has staff with particular responsibility for formulating and developing disability policy.

Essential elements in the job of the 'disability specialists' in organisations A and C include providing information and advice, whilst also helping managers and supervisors acquire skills and confidence in disability-related issues. In neither of the organisations is the disability specialist in direct contact with most employees with disabilities, in part because of the inadequacy of resources.

Why should Organisations have a Policy with Resources allocated to Disability Issues at Work?

The research suggests a variety of reasons why organisations should develop more active policies, for example:

- most organisations are not fulfilling their legal requirement to employ a minimum of 3% of registered disabled people.

- in the two researched organisations with more active policies, people are successfully employed who would not otherwise have been recruited. Some are in jobs where, because of a disability, they might not have been considered in many organisations.

- the research also revealed examples of problems at work which were described as arising from, or related to, an individual's disability but which could have arisen with any employee with or without a disability. Misconceptions and, on occasions, prejudice, can result in managers assuming that a particular disability has resulted in a problem. An active disability policy will address the misconceptions and stereotypes surrounding disability, which stand in the way of the employment of people with disabilities in jobs which use their skills and knowledge, and develop their potential.

- in all organisations employees become temporarily or permanently disabled. A bad back or a heart attack is not a rare occurrence. Such disabilities can severely handicap an individual in their current job, either short- or long-term, and their employer is faced with the decision as to what to do with them whilst they are incapacitated. Although organisations have formal policies relating to sick leave entitlement and retirement on medical grounds, few have policies relating to the assessment and rehabilitation of employees.

- an active disability management policy is particularly needed at times of change. Many work situations involving an employee with a disability are well managed - by the individual, and perhaps their supervisor and managers, and their colleagues - until a change occurs. A change of supervisor or manager, of technology, of location, of task, of work priorities, of workflow, or a refurbishment of a building, affects all employees, but particularly those with a disability. It is at times of change that a supervisor or manager, or the person with a disability, may be in most need of advice, information, or assistance to forestall or minimise the negative effects of such changes.

- there are only small numbers of people with relatively severe disabilities in any organisation. Like any minority, for example ethnic minorities, or women in non-traditional jobs, they may feel isolated. An active policy can help put those who want contact in touch with others in a similar situation.

The needs of managers and supervisors for advice and information on disability issues can, of course, be met without creating a formal policy. However a policy, with resources to implement it, means that steps can be taken to be proactive rather than reactive in promoting more effective disability management.

Chapter 5

Summary of Recommendations for Improving Practice in 'Open Employment' Organisations

Training

The following recommendations take account of the organisational constraints discussed in Chapter 3.

We recommend special disability training for the following:

- all trainers

- staff formally responsible for disability issues in the organisation whether in personnel, welfare or medical roles

- anyone selecting staff or involved in recruiting

- a manager or supervisor before they become responsible for supervising an employee with a disability

- all staff with disabilities.

We also recommend that:

- all management and supervisory, customer care and interpersonal skills courses should contain elements on disability management

- all other staff should be given the opportunity and be encouraged to attend short sessions on disability

- all training should involve an interactive element and, where possible, specialist trainers and staff with disabilities should be involved.

Disability Policy

We recommend the development of an active disability policy which includes the following elements:

- the policy statement should make clear what actions will be taken, by whom and when

- the person, or people responsible for developing and monitoring the policy should be specified

- people with disabilities should be consulted and involved, in appropriate ways, in the development and monitoring of the policy;

- the policy should be communicated to all staff in ways which make clear to them their role in its implementation

- the operation of the policy should be monitored regularly by a representative group including senior management

- training should be provided for all key groups of employees, and information on disability given to all others

- sufficient resources should be allocated to disability issues to ensure all the above can be done, on a continuous basis.

Part III

Improving Practice In
A Sheltered Employment Organisation

Chapter 6

The Research in Remploy

In this, Part 3, we shall present an analysis of our fundings in Remploy.

The Views of Staff on the Need for Managers and Supervisors in Remploy to have Greater Knowledge of Disability Issues

Many of the managers and supervisors interviewed felt that their knowledge and understanding of physical and other disabilities was inadequate for coping with many of the situations they faced, a view shared by non-supervisory staff. The main areas of concern related to productivity, safety, discipline and employee development.

Productivity

'In Remploy we need to know people's ability and potential in order to know what production can reasonably be fulfilled. But we also need to know about how their disability would affect them.'

Supervisor with disability

Safety

'I'm terrified of doing the wrong thing - putting the wrong person in the wrong job. At the moment the factory doctor really determines who can use what equipment by making his medical reports. I would like the knowledge to determine myself who should use which equipment and what kinds of work people can do. I shouldn't have to wait until the accident happens to find out.'

Manager without disability

Discipline

> '*Another problem is knowing how firm to be. I really don't know how much firmness is appropriate with different individuals and in different situations.*'

> > Manager without disability

Employee Development

> '*Because we are afraid to push too hard .. so many disabled people are denied the opportunity to develop. They're not given the chance to demonstrate what they can do.*'

> > Supervisor without disability

The need was also expressed for different kinds of information:

- how to deal with *specific situations;*

> '*I would like some training in communication skills. I get embarrassed with people who are deaf and dumb - I have mental blockages - can't think of ways of getting across to them. And I can't think of the right words to use with other people, the right level of communication.*'

> > Manager without disability

- information about certain *types of disability;*

> '*I'd like to know how to identify triggering mechanisms, for example in cases of epilepsy or schizophrenia. It would help me to know how to avoid problems.*'

> > Manager without disability

- information about an *individual's disability;*

> '*I had to make a nuisance of myself to find out. People are here because they have complaints, and we need the information because we have responsibilities.*'

> > Supervisor without disability

Situations requiring Disability Management

Perhaps the most striking finding to emerge from our research is the extent to which the need for a greater knowledge and understanding of disabilities extends to almost the entire range of supervisory concerns.

Foremost amongst them, of course, is the concern with *maintaining a safe working environment.*

If a supervisor has inadequate knowledge of a disability they may well ask workers to do tasks where they will be exposed to unacceptable and unnecessary hazards, or they may put at risk other fellow workers. Conversely, they may fear a danger which does not in fact exist, and underutilise staff resources.

Maintaining and improving performance requires that people are allocated to the most appropriate jobs, that they are trained effectively, that their performance is monitored, and that employee motivation is stimulated and sustained. Without adequate knowledge of the implications of disabilities, there is a danger of inappropriate assessment and selection techniques being used, or of individuals not being given the most appropriate targets, equipment or level of supervision.

These views were shared by staff who are not themselves managing or supervising staff. A factory doctor said:

> *'My main complaint, as factory doctor, is that someone starts on a Monday and does not have a medical until Thursday, so it's a management decision where that person works. I do sometimes feel that people have been put on the wrong jobs.'*

An operative with a disability said:

> *'The jobs (on the other section) were different and I had to keep a different pace with different jobs. Sometimes they were complicated and needed more speed than I can manage, and I found it hard to figure out where the lines were. Sometimes I asked to try different jobs because the one I was on was too difficult and I was told just to do the best I could, but I knew I was not doing it properly because I was only doing one to their three.'*

A closely related area is that of *employee development,* in which the supervisor has a prime responsibility to be able to recognise untapped potential and to create conditions which allow it to develop. Without a proper understanding of the possible effects of a disability, a supervisor may all too easily make incorrect assumptions about an individual's potential.

> *'When a blind person started here someone came in to help him. We had never had a blind person in the factory before. He was given an assembly job to do, assembling three-point plugs. We put him on it and when we found he could do it we just forgot about him. We assumed he couldn't do anything more complicated. Other people were assembling lamps, which seemed very complicated because there were a lot of different parts. When we ran out of the plug job*

we didn't know what to try him on. I decided to let him have a go at the lamps just to see. He produced more than the others. Since then I have tried him on practically everything. Now he is able to work several machines.'

Superintendent without disability

Knowledge of the disability is equally important when it comes to *avoiding and dealing with potential crises and problems.* The supervisor, in particular, has to know when an individual needs more time to learn a new task because of a learning disability or difficulties with reading instructions. They need to be able to avoid placing individuals in situations which might exacerbate their condition, or in for example the case of epilepsy, actually trigger a seizure. They also have to be able to defuse problem situations when they do arise, recognise possible reasons for under-achievement and be aware, in particular, of the possible side-effects of medication.

'I do have good and bad days. When I first had my nervous breakdown I had shock treatment which made me lose my memory for a long time. Then I was put on injections. I had them 3-weekly, so then I used to have one good week and I would gradually go down over the next two weeks. It used to make me exhausted and I had an awful chip on my shoulder. Now I have been taken off the injections and put onto tablets. I take the tablets more regularly and it keeps me more even. My supervisor is a marvellous man to have about. He is like a Dutch uncle to me. But it would help if people here knew a bit more to understand the helplessness of depression.'

Operative with disability

A full appreciation of the effects of a disability on an employee is equally important when it comes to *making disciplinary decisions.* The factory superintendent, and to a lesser degree the supervisor, is frequently faced with the dilemma of deciding whether someone is genuinely unable to work faster or whether they are 'lead-swinging.' Similarly they must make judgements as to whether lateness or absence is justified or not.

'In three cases I have asked our doctor to contact a person's GP. On one occasion a person's supervisor asked them to do a job that he'd done in the past. On that day he said he couldn't do it because he couldn't bend down. On his form it said 'deaf and dumb' but there was obviously something else. We just didn't know what it was. The GP wrote back to say there was a terminal illness. He wouldn't give us any more information than that, and probably the individual concerned did not know about it. I decided not to put him back on the job which he had complained of. I would not force him to do

a job but I would leave it up to him to say he couldn't do it. The problem is that if someone says 'no' to a job, twenty other people will also say "no" to it. That puts immense problems on the supervisor.'

Superintendent without disability

'In the morning I need extra time for my legs to come round, for them to come back to life. I often just make it in in the morning by the skin of my teeth.'

Operative with disability

'I had a problem in the other section when I had just arrived. I did not understand the person's problem. It was my first week. I lost my temper with someone. He looks such a big healthy person. I must have told him to sweep the floor or something like that, because he said he could not stand the dust flying about. I thought he was lazy. When I found out that he had only one lung I became much more sympathetic, but I should have been told that when I started.'

Supervisor with disability

Training, induction, and coaching is another area in which an understanding of disability is essential if the most effective training methods are to be selected and equipment, adaptations or other assistance provided. Allowance must also be made for the different amounts of time that may be needed to learn a job.

'It takes me longer than a completely sighted person to learn something new. I have to find out my own ways of doing things. The supervisor cannot see through your eyes. He does not know the best way to show you. For example when I was doing labelling I was told to line things up by the lettering, but I could not see the actual lettering properly. I found that if I held the labels up I could see the difference between the light and dark parts and I could line these up together, but I had to let the light reflect onto it. I have to be near either sunlight or artificial light, the brighter the light the better. An anglepoise lamp with a reflector bulb would probably be very helpful for anyone with poor eyesight, but we do not have any of those.'

Operative with disability

Supervisors and managers must be able to *communicate* with their employees and ensure that other fellow-workers make provision for the special communication needs of employees with speech and hearing difficulties.

'Communication problems mean that it is hard to delegate. There's a wealth of information I'd like to give out, but it's hard. One leading hand is deaf without speech, so I have to give him written information. But another is dyslexic, so I can't give him the same written information - it has to be verbal. People have to be communicated with in different forms and at different levels of complexity.'

Manager without disability

The supervisor also needs a proper understanding of people's disabilities in order to *assemble and build a team* whose abilities complement each other and meet the requirements of the job. This is an important part of a supervisor's job in any organisation, but in sheltered employment it is particularly important that supervisors recognise, build on and use people's strengths whilst taking account of their disabilities. This requires special and unusual skills and knowledge.

'It's very important to consider what people you are going to put on a job because of the needs of each job. It's also important to put the right combination of people together. Some people can't stand, some can't bend down, and some can't lift. So I do need to know about their disability.'

Superintendent without disability

Supervisors also need to be able to recognise when to discourage someone from being over-helpful or solicitous towards a fellow-worker.

'Other people spoil me terribly. They help me much more than is necessary. They think I cannot do things which I perfectly well can. I do not tell them not to do it even if I can do it, because I do not like to hurt their feelings.'

Operative with disability

Supervisors must know too *when to summon assistance* from a first aider or refer someone to the factory doctor. Here again a proper knowledge and understanding of the disability is vital.

'I don't really know at what point to get an ambulance - only with those people I happen to know about. For example the man on my section with a heart condition cut his hand. He went to the gents and collapsed. He cut his head open and it was bleeding profusely. I knew he takes a drug for his heart condition which stops blood clotting. So I called an ambulance straight away. I know about the

people on my section because I've asked them. But I don't know about the people on other sections, even though I'm a first aider.'

Supervisor with disability

Remploy managers and supervisors are often required to *recognise and deal with employees' problems.* Again, knowledge of the disability is often crucial.

'You have to carefully expose people to stress situations, where they are vulnerable to stress. It's not just epilepsy. People with other disabilities are handicapped in that way. But if you can get them through the difficult time they will often turn out to be a useful and profitable employee. This is one of the experiences we can help industry with generally. If you can only give them the opportunity and help them through that initial phase, frequently they are among your best.'

Supervisor without disability

The Need for Knowledge About Certain Types of Disability

As the previous section illustrates, the effective management of a situation often requires a greater understanding of disability issues than many managers and supervisors currently feel they have. *Newly appointed managers and supervisors,* especially those with little or no previous experience of working with people with a range of different types of disability, frequently need the reassurance which increased knowledge can provide.

'I was apprenticed at another factory. That company folded up. Interviews were always after hours, so I didn't know that people here were disabled until I started to work here. I found it very hard to start with. It took time to get used to them, especially to the mentally handicapped people. It was like being a teacher. After a few months I decided to look elsewhere. I was offered a higher position if I stayed on, and I agreed. I was used to outside employment, and it took a lot of adapting to.'

Supervisor without disability

More experienced staff also feel the need for training to advise them whether the disability management strategies they have developed, sometimes over many years, are the most effective.

'We in Remploy have a lot of experience, but that doesn't mean it's the best experience. My concern is how we strengthen the ability

> *of our supervisors to cope with very wide-ranging demands asso-*
> *ciated with many different disabilities.'*

Manager without disability

In some cases information is needed in order to *dispel misconceptions* about the implications of a disability.

> *'So many problems disabled people experience are due to ignorance*
> *on the part of the rest of us. How can you help people who are at*
> *the sharp end of the employment business, the charge hands and*
> *the foremen who may be reacting to the label "epilepsy" or "schi-*
> *zophrenia"?'*

Supervisor without disability

In many instances where managers and supervisors experience difficulties arising from a particular type of disability, there is a need for *specific information relating to that disability*. For example, more effective management of hearing and speech impairment may include knowledge of ways of facilitating lip reading and improving communication in order to reduce misunderstandings, frustration and isolation.

> *'Some people talk too quickly, or if they don't open their mouths*
> *properly it is difficult to lip read. People often talk with a cigarette*
> *in their mouth, while they are chewing a sweet or something like*
> *that, or they don't stand and face you directly. If they need to attract*
> *my attention they sometimes throw something. They sometimes*
> *bang on the table, clap or touch me. I feel vibrations if people bang.'*

Supervisor with disability

The management of other types of disability may also require more specific knowledge, for example of different forms of epilepsy.

Guidance in ways of dealing with behaviour problems, as well as information about the *behaviours associated with a disability*, may help to increase confidence in managing particularly difficult situations.

> *'I'd have liked to have been told beforehand how to handle people*
> *with schizophrenia. It would have helped to have been told that they*
> *go up and down, that this isn't your fault, that you didn't do*
> *something wrong. How to react to difficult behaviour or even*
> *violence. Be firm? Try to calm them down?'*

Operative with disability

The Need for Information about an Employee's Disability

Providing supervisors and managers with training to increase their knowledge and understanding of disabilities in general will only be of value if they also know the specific disabilities experienced by the individual workers for whom they are responsible. The assumption is sometimes made that because many supervisory staff in Remploy themselves have disabilities, they will have the experience to manage disability at work more effectively. However, supervisors interviewed, whether or not they themselves have a disability, stressed the need for greater knowledge and skills to improve their own disability management, and to enable them to help others manage disability more confidently. It is in the area of obtaining information about people they supervise or manage that those interviewed expressed their strongest concerns with regard to the current situation in Remploy.

Nearly every supervisor interviewed, together with one of the superintendents, said that they needed to be given much more information on the disabilities of their workers.

Even more surprising was the fact that the first aid officers said they were not provided with the information they needed. First aiders also felt the need to know about the medication workers were on.

In the absence of a more formal system to meet these needs, supervisors and first aid officers may have to rely upon whatever information they can obtain from the individuals themselves. A first aider said 'It is up to them to tell me or the charge hand what they cannot do', but a supervisor said that he 'never asked people about their condition' and felt the need to know 'what procedure there is for finding out.'

Obtaining information only from the individual with the disability is not in any case always going to be satisfactory. One worker stated that he 'wouldn't like to tell people what I cannot do, because then they wouldn't give me a chance to try things.' One of the superintendents similarly pointed out that employees were 'reluctant to tell the whole truth'. A further difficulty that may arise in this regard is, according to several managers and supervisors, that focussing on an individual's disabilities may go against the whole 'culture' in Remploy.

> 'Disability awareness has never come up at any management training session as far as I know. Normality is important. We try to be as normal as possible on the shop floor. That's why we run it as far as possible as a normal business.'

> Manager without disability

Some people we interviewed are concerned about focusing on disability issues because they feel that their factory has been successful by concentrating on ability. Others suggest that greater understanding of disability issues will ultimately enable abilities to be developed and utilised more effectively.

A closely related issue is the attitude to what are termed 'secondary disabilities.' This expression is sometimes used to mean disabilities which only come to light after a worker has been employed for some time. (The term 'secondary disabilities' should strictly be used only to describe disabilities which develop as a consequence of a primary disability, and it might actually be better, and more accurate, to refer to 'undisclosed disabilities'). One of the managers stated *'We're not very sympathetic to secondary disabilities'*, but a superintendent acknowledged that they often pose a serious problem and this was confirmed by several supervisors.

> *'We're not told about people's secondary disabilities. I have a deaf boy without speech. No one said he has cerebral palsy. He copes with the deafness, but his cerebral palsy causes the problems.'*

Supervisor with disability

Sometimes it is not a 'secondary disability' but a secondary factor arising from the disability, such as low self-esteem or reluctance to accept a change of work status, which can cause difficulties both for the individual and supervisory staff.

> *'Ours is a mining community. There are no other job opportunities. It's all physical manual work. So it's even more difficult to cope with even minor disabilities. It makes people feel inadequate. This can be a greater problem than the physical disability itself.'*

Supervisor without disability

> *'One man with a heart problem was not prepared to accept that he had a disability. He had a chip on his shoulder. He was very dogmatic about what he was prepared to do. He was used to doing more important work in his previous employment. The supervisor needs to know how to handle someone like that.'*

Supervisor without disability

It has to be recognised that, while there may be a good deal of scope for sharing existing information more effectively, in many cases adequate information on an individual's condition and how it affects them at work simply does not exist. A first aid officer pointed out that *'often people arrive here without a medical report'*. One of the factory doctors confirmed that there were *'problems in getting enough medical information . . . I receive nothing when the person starts. I get nothing from the DRO . . . I write to the GP, but many GPs are not co-operative and do not reply.'* For some reason these problems seem to be worse in Remploy than in other companies with which this doctor worked.

It is also necessary to point out that better medical information on workers' conditions on its own would not meet the requirements of supervisors and managers. Information is also needed on how the condition actually affects the ability of the individual to carry out the various tasks they might have to do in the factory. This points to the need for a more thorough and comprehensive assessment of individuals before they are allocated to a job. At one factory, an assessment centre had once existed which had been used by a number of factories to assess some potential recruits. It was suggested that its use was limited because it did not reflect *'the actual work done in the factory - the tasks that were involved were not closely enough linked to the work on the factory floor.'* (Supervisor without disability).

Chapter 7

Developing Training in Remploy

Staff Views on Training

Before considering how training might be developed to meet the needs identified, it will be helpful to consider first some of the views of those we interviewed regarding the kind of training they felt would be most useful.

The majority of those interviewed said they would welcome the opportunity of learning about disability-related issues as they felt this would enable them to cope with situations more effectively. They also felt the need for specific information about certain types of disability. Several were quite clear, however, that they did not want

> 'a lot of medical information . . . what the charge hand needs to know is how the disability may affect the person and how to deal with situations that arise'

Supervisor with disability

The suggestion was made that a considerable amount of the information needed about disabilities could be obtained from the individuals with the disability, if supervisors could be given the opportunity and guidance in how to broach a sensitive subject and appropriate questions to ask.

> 'After all, we need to provide the assistance the disabled person wants, not what we think they need.'

Manager without disability

A senior manager pointed out that supervisors would not want 'to be lectured at for hours at a time . . . they need to go out and do something in groups or on the shop floor. You have to use actual case histories.' One manager agreed that 'information must be presented simply and in pictorial form where possible.' Another felt that in training 'you need to reproduce real-life situations.' A superintendent thought that group discussions are helpful for people who have been in the job for some time.

The importance of the training venue was also stressed. The senior manager believed that any supervisory training should be done in the factory. A supervisor, however, said she had missed most of a training session held in the factory because she was continually being called out to deal with problems on the shop floor.

A senior manager also emphasised the need to integrate any disability management training into other supervisory training. This view was echoed by one of the superintendents, who said:

> *'I think disability training could be incorporated into all the other training, and would make the other training much more useful and appropriate, but you must be careful not to generalise about disabilities or about people.'*

Superintendent without disability

A related issue is that of who should provide the training. Should it be done by factory staff, for example first aid officers, or by trainers from outside? One manager felt that whoever did the training needed to have a good knowledge of Remploy, otherwise the training would be too theoretical. He stressed, too, the need for training to have *'continuity . . . it needs to be ongoing to have any effect.'* Another manager also pointed to the risk of people *'forgetting what it was all about'* if there is too large a break between training sessions. The divisional manager suggested that each training session should be limited to half a day and that the supervisors should then be able to go out into the factory *'to do something practical.'*

The role of distance learning was also discussed. It was agreed that this might be a good way of meeting the needs of managers in this area.

Meeting the Training Needs of Managers

It is essential that a disability element is integrated into *all managerial training and training for factory superintendents,* and specifically that a disability management module is developed to supplement the Open University 'Effective Manager' distance learning package, which is currently in use for a selected group of new and potential managers within Remploy. The following are areas where the management of disability needs to be given priority: business development; recruitment and selection; job allocation; staff development; safety, to include practical implications of responsibilities under the Health and Safety at Work Act (see Chapter 10).

More training in *selection and interviewing* needs to be provided for those recruiting people with disabilities. This would help minimise stress to applicants and recruiters and avoid inappropriate questions and task allocation. Some managers may also benefit from guidance in establishing a more satisfactory working relationship with their DROs.

> *'People are recommended by the DRO, who has been told what the work entails but who sometimes sends completely unsuitable people. One woman spent £12 on a taxi to come to the interview. She had cerebral palsy and couldn't even pick up a screwdriver. It was a crime to send her - it raised her hopes when she just couldn't do the job.'*
>
> Manager without disability

Meeting the Training Needs of Supervisors

It is evident that there is also an urgent need for disability management to become an important part of the supervisory training programme which is being developed within Remploy, and for:

- disability management to be integrated into all supervisory training

- such supervisory training to be made available to all those with, and with the potential to undertake, supervisory responsibilities, including charge hands and leading hands

- trainers who are involved in providing such training to have a deep understanding of disability issues and of Remploy, in order that the training provided is directly relevant

- such training to be highly participative, informal, and based on Remploy situations, using Remploy case studies where appropriate

- training to include the management implications of certain types of disability. Such training must involve, as part of the trainer team, Remploy employees at any level who have the disability under discussion.

- training to take place in premises which have training equipment and facilities, but which are not intimidating.

It was suggested by a number of people that everyone in a supervisory capacity should have some basic *first aid training* (to include dealing with common situations, such as an epileptic seizure).

Supervisory staff and others involved in training should be given training in how to *train and coach others,* including how to train people with special needs. Not all are as confident or assured as this trainer:

> *'On one instructional techniques course I asked for a volunteer to whom I would teach a task, as a demonstration. A man with one hand came forward challenging me to teach him. I had to say I didn't know how, but that I would go away and find out. That night I went home and taught myself how to do the task with one hand. The next day I went back and taught the volunteer.'*

More emphasis might also be given to increasing the provision of more systematic training for all present and potential supervisors. Management of the probationary period and the monitoring of progress are seen as particularly important but neglected areas at present.

> *'The supervisors in this factory are not really acting as supervisors. They set machines and then become machine minders. There is a tremendous need for proper supervisory training. Unless this is done, disability management training will not be as effective as it should be.'*

Manager without disability

It was also pointed out that supervisors who regard their role as 'machine experts' are too insecure to pass on their knowledge to others.

Meeting the Training Needs of Other Groups

Supervisory training could be extended to *leading hands* and others with the desire and potential to undertake supervisory responsibilities.

> *'My leading hand is an excellent worker - he should be getting training so he can become a supervisor. But it won't happen unless I die or retire. He won't receive any training at all unless he becomes a charge hand, and his only chance of that is by getting some training, so it's a vicious circle.'*

Supervisor with disability

Official first aid officers should have supplementary training, as many think that the training they receive is inadequate for Remploy's needs (for example, their training does not cover the side effects of medication or the possible consequences of not taking prescribed medication).

Other specific groups have been identified who would benefit from training on aspects of managing disability:

- all new employees

- safety officers

- production engineers

- sales representatives

- union representatives

- all those involved in interviewing, selection, and counselling.

Meeting the Training Needs of all Employees

It is crucial that disability management is recognised as being, first and foremost, the responsibility of the individual employee with the disability. It is important, therefore, that some training on managing disability be given to all employees.

> *'I would love to have any training I could get on disability. I can do a bit of sign language, because I went to help at a club for deaf and dumb people. The more information you get about people's disabilities the better. You can accept people a lot more if you know about their disabilities. Outwardly they sometimes don't show any disability but they may be very angry inside. You can help calm them down if you know.'*

Operative with disability

Change of trade in a factory or the introduction of new processes are occasions when skills training for all staff is necessary. Examples were given of only specific operatives being selected for trade skills training, and of inappropriate training being given, for example by non-English speaking machinery suppliers. We therefore recommend that *trade skills training* be more widely available, and that such training be monitored to ensure that it is appropriate.

Some people with disabilities would benefit from *assertiveness training*.

> *'Sometimes if it's a job they don't like they pretend they don't understand me. Because I am deaf and dumb some people resent being told what to do by me.'*

Supervisor with disability

> *'Parents do not do their children any favours by overprotecting them. For some people the loss of parents is very traumatic and they need to go through a training period to learn to cope.'*

Supervisor without disability

Training in numeracy and literacy may be required by some.

'It's difficult to judge some people's intelligence level. Some people underestimate others. Then you have the person who comes in with a newspaper under his arm. He can't read, but he listens to the radio or to the others talking and then repeats what he's heard as if he's read it in the paper. You don't find out he's illiterate until something happens. I put notices all over the machine saying "Do not turn on." Then I was lying under it trying to get it sorted out and he went and turned it on. It wasn't any good being angry - he couldn't read the notices. But I didn't know he couldn't until that happened. Now I make it my business to find out straight away who can read and who can write. I found that of the 14 people then on my section, only two were able to read "Do not touch" correctly.'

Supervisor without disability

Chapter 8

Organisational Issues in Remploy

Introduction

Improving the management of disability at work does not only mean providing staff with the kind of training outlined in the previous chapter. It also requires that a number of other, organisational issues are addressed.

In the course of our research in Remploy our attention was drawn to a number of such issues. In many instances the need for Remploy to change its practices in certain respects was pointed out. At the same time, though, a number of Remploy practices were mentioned as already making a significant contribution to better disability management.

As was noted earlier, in the preface, some of the issues that were raised were clearly peculiar to Remploy - issues such as its image and the way in which its business was being developed. Others, though, we felt were likely to have a wider relevance. In this chapter we shall therefore describe some of these organisational issues.

Personnel Procedures

A number of issues relating to *recruitment and selection* were raised. Two staff members from one factory who had been recruited after replying to job advertisements, which did not mention disability or make it clear that Remploy offers sheltered employment, both felt that all advertisements should contain such information in order to avoid stress and the possibility of people leaving soon after recruitment.

Several employees who attended panel interviews reported finding them particularly stressful. Panel interviews are no longer carried out at all factories.

Clarification was requested by a supervisor on whether a person is recruited into Remploy for a specific job, or whether:

> 'People who come to work in a Remploy factory have to be prepared to do whatever job they are given.'

It was suggested by several of those interviewed that before *induction* of a new employee takes place, information should be made available to the person carrying out the induction regarding the individual's previous work experience, any communication difficulties, and any other information relevant to the induction process.

Induction, it was suggested, should include a discussion between the individual and the supervisor or charge hand about the person's strengths, weaknesses and work preferences.

It was felt that some job rotation should be included during the probationary period.

Some of those interviewed were of the opinion that having a disability reduces prospects of *promotion* within Remploy, while others were of the opinion that *not* having a disability reduces both promotion and long-term security prospects.

As previously mentioned, it was suggested that promotion into supervisory roles is frustrated because of lack of training. An additional factor was thought to be the lack of a standardised role and status for leading hands, some of whom are running sections while others are seen by supervisors as *'the better workers, but with no extra responsibility.'* Assumptions about the responsibilities of leading hands sometimes result in people with certain types of disability being thought unsuitable for promotion.

> *'I have mentioned to the superintendent that some of the deaf people should become leading hands, but he seemed to think not, that it will not happen simply because you have to be able to communicate with everyone as a leading hand. Also they may not understand how to fill in the work sheets, and it may take longer for them to learn.'*

> Supervisor with disability

Such assumptions were clearly not justified, as those interviewed included a supervisor and a leading hand who were both deaf and had impaired speech.

Although recognising that increasing numbers of people with disabilities are being promoted, a number of people did mention the lack of formal and regular *assessment* and that they knew of little systematic *career development*.

On the other hand, it was felt that other companies could learn a good deal from Remploy with regard to the way in which it stressed abilities rather than disabilities. Thus, whereas in open employment an experienced older worker who becomes disabled may be retired early on medical grounds, in Remploy the skills of such a person are recognised and utilised even if they have reduced strength and mobility.

> *'I worked for 31 years in a printing firm. My work was too hard for me. I have difficulty walking and lifting and there was too much standing. Now in Remploy I supervise 14 or 15 people. I can sit because most of the people are doing bench work. I am also the Safety Officer and I do safety induction for everyone. On my Safety Officer's course I had an opportunity to discuss with others who were also new to Remploy, and I found that I had a lot less difficulty adjusting than some of the other people. I related that to having trained apprentices outside.'*

Supervisor with disability

Working hours were also mentioned by several of those interviewed. Although a number of them regretted that no part-time working is available in Remploy (and some would have found this particularly helpful, for example after a spell in hospital), several commented that because factories select their own hours of work they are able to avoid travelling during the rush hours by early starting and finishing. In some cases this further example of Remploy good practice has enabled people with deteriorating conditions to continue working, for example one man with cerebral palsy commented:

> *'The journey to work is very hard. I have to come by train and bus. I like to get in early so I can have a rest before I start work. I have waited an hour for a bus, and that is no fun in the winter. But if I had to do it in the rush hour, I just wouldn't manage it.'*

Another area of good practice in Remploy which a factory doctor commented upon is the facility with which someone is able to be transferred to a different type of work, either temporarily or permanently, if their physical condition makes this necessary. This is especially important for those with fluctuating or deteriorating conditions. An example is a man with a chest complaint who commented *'If I have a particularly bad day I can do a sitting down job.'* Other companies might also emulate the way in which Remploy teams up people with different disabilities, so that together they can do a job which on their own they would be unable to do.

Safety Procedures

There was some uncertainty about the extent to which employees have the 'right' to choose to undertake potentially hazardous tasks. The chief first aider in one factory referred to a man with epilepsy who *'if you molly-coddle him will have a fit simply because you are causing him frustration. I let him climb ladders and everything.'* The safety officer in the same factory was adamant that people at risk should not be permitted to carry out such tasks:

> *'It's always the employer's responsibility. The employees cannot take chances for themselves. I would jeopardise my own job if they had an accident, as well as their safety.'*

Many of Remploy's safety procedures, however, might well be adopted much more widely:

- the designation of a supervisor to be responsible for the evacuation of employees with mobility problems

- timed fire drills with checks on reasons for the slowness of individual sections

- designation of someone to be responsible for the evacuation of deaf people

- a conveyor belt to remove rubbish so that the factory floor is free of obstacles

- coloured lines on the shop floor indicating passageways to be kept free

- stressing of safety when choosing and installing machines

- making a signer available for the safety induction of an employee with a hearing disability

- strict smoking restrictions applied also to visitors.

Although such practices are not unique to Remploy, the heightened awareness of potential hazards both inside and outside the factory results in action being taken at all levels to create as safe a working environment as possible.

> *'I've even seen the Manager go out himself and put sand down on the snow, so they're really very caring.'*

Operative with disability

Aids and Adaptations

Many Remploy supervisors are very creative with regard to designing adaptations for individuals with special needs. For example:

- using lengths of cardboard to extend a workbench for someone with arthritis

131

· providing a box to support a leg or foot.

Several people, however, suggested that those working in sheltered employment should also have access to the range of aids and adaptations made available to people with disabilities who are in open employment.

Health and Welfare

Concern was expressed about the amount of *health cover* available at factories. But this was countered by a management view that Remploy factories are, as far as is possible, ordinary working places and should therefore not have more medical cover than any other workplace. These conflicting views are reflected by the fact that although each factory has regular visits from a doctor, there is no standardised minimum duration for doctors' sessions. There was considerable discrepancy between the time the two doctors interviewed spent at their respective factories, and the duties they were therefore able to perform.

One factory doctor reported:

> *'One hour a week is totally inadequate. It is not possible to give people thorough regular medicals twice a year . . . the majority are only seen once a year. It means tests cannot be done.'*

Another factory doctor spent between two hours and half a day a week in his factory and made a point of staying to lunch every week *'so that people know I am available'*. Everyone in this factory had a medical twice a year, and the kitchens and WCs were regularly inspected, as hygiene was seen as part of this doctor's wide-ranging responsibilities.

> *'I see myself very much as part of the Remploy team. I often go to study a problem at the bench, and have made recommendations in the light of the actual work situation for a change of work, for a different chair, bench, or more light, or for workers to be moved if their personalities clash.'*

Mention has already been made of the fact that first aiders did not think they received either *sufficient information about individuals,* or training adequate for Remploy's needs.

However, in one factory the chief first aider was a member of both the Absence Committee (which monitors punctuality and attendance) and the Health and Safety Committee. The manager reported that this first aider sees the doctor every Thursday and they discuss people's disabilities and decide together if the person can do the job. *'He knows more about medical things than I do.'* The doctor confirmed that she relied on the first aider for information.

> *'The first aider in this factory is very good. He is a supervisor who has been here for a long time, so he knows everyone well. He is able to tell me about the individuals and about the jobs and we work well together. I don't know if the system would work as well with another first aider who was less experienced and knowledgeable.'*

Another first aider had received first aid training a year previously, and felt the course gave her *'a lot more confidence. . . . I think all supervisors and leading hands here should have first aid training.'* This was a view expressed by a number of other supervisory staff, including first aiders in other factories.

Welfare is regarded by some as a key aspect of the Remploy supervisory role, but other managers say no more emphasis should be placed on it than in any factory in industry. However, those interviewed frequently mentioned having inadequate knowledge or time to give as much help as they would like. A retired supervisor said:

> *'I used to look after welfare here. Sometimes people have housing problems. I quite often used to be in touch with social workers. Some of the people live on their own or in hostels. They need someone to talk to, get advice from. I have had quite a lot of contact with people's GPs. No-one has taken over my welfare role. Supervisors, the office people, and the factory managers sometimes have to do some of these things, but I think it is a pity there is no-one special.'*

The lack of regular *staffing of the first aid room* was another concern for some people. One man said he stood by the fire escape *'so they can see me from the factory'* rather than go to the unstaffed first aid room when he felt unwell. Others mentioned sitting to recover on the shop floor rather than going to an unstaffed room. If the first aid officer were called out to attend to someone in the first aid room, their own section would often be left unsupervised with possible productivity consequences. One first aider described how she arranged for a red light to be fitted outside the door of the first aid room because:

> *'I have had people who have become violent in there, and when you are on your own it is very frightening. I had someone who I really could not contain. I had to get help from the shop floor, so I had two choices. I had to leave him alone while I got help or cope with him on my own. Now anyone going by would see the red light on and call another first aider or any supervisor.'*

Other points raised were that there was usually *no designated person to monitor the taking of medication,* although people with mental illness in particular are sometimes felt to be not able to manage their own medication. These differences seem to point to a need for some standardisation of health cover in order to increase both safety and productivity, and the smooth running of factories.

Chapter 9

The Wider Implications of the Research in Sheltered Employment

Introduction

In Part III, we have so far confined ourselves to an examination of training needs and organisational issues in Remploy. In this final chapter we shall consider the wider implications of our research for other organisations providing sheltered work.

Organisations providing Sheltered Work

Although we have not yet investigated training needs in sheltered workshops managed by other organisations, anecdotal and impressionistic knowledge of a number of other workshops would suggest that there is no reason to suspect that their needs would be very different from those of Remploy. Furthermore, the second largest provider of sheltered employment (after Remploy) is the Spastics Society, which has been one of our collaborating partners.

We would therefore recommend that all organisations responsible for the operation of sheltered workshops improve their training of staff by:

- integrating disability management training into all aspects of management and supervisory training

- ensuring that those responsible for providing such training have a deep understanding of disability issues

- involving disabled employees in the provision of such training

- basing the training on case-studies which illustrate the work experiences of disabled employees, ideally drawn from the organisation itself

- arranging for some training on managing disability to be given to all employees.

As in the case of Remploy, we would stress the need for supporting such training initiatives by improved personnel practices such as:

- the informed and responsible interpretation and use of the information on employees' disabilities and medication that is obtained from Disablement Resettlement Officers and occupational physicians

- drawing up clear guidelines on who has access to this information

- introducing regular reviews of employees' work performance and aspirations and monitoring their progress

- giving employees the opportunity to demonstrate their potential by placing them in a wide variety of different job situations.

Finally, as in the case of Remploy, we believe there are a number of other ways in which the management of disabilities can be made more effective in sheltered workshops:

- by gearing the development of new products or services to the abilities and potential of their employees

- by publicising the achievements of successful employees, who can act as 'role models' for other employees and help dispel managers' misconceptions

- by setting up a proper vocational assessment and guidance service

- by providing an adequate occupational health service.

Other Organisations

There are also ways in which other organisations, not directly involved in the provision of sheltered work, might contribute to better disability management. We would like to see:

- the development of supplementary materials on disability management for the nationally recognised training programmes for supervisors

- the development of a disability management module to supplement the Open University's 'Effective Manager' distance learning package

- the development of a Code of Practice for sheltered workshops, similar to that produced by the Department of Employment for organisations providing open employment

- the establishment of training courses on 'Managing Disability at Work'

- the preparation of a handbook on the possible implications of a variety of types of disability on employment, which brings together the information contained in RADAR's excellent *Employers' Guide*, the United States Department of Labour's Disability Guidance notes, and other sources of such information.

Appendix 1

Collaborating Partners

Confederation of British Industry *

Inner London Education Authority *

Institute of Personnel Management *

Legal and General Insurance Group

Local Government Training Board *

London Boroughs' Disability Resource Team *

Midland Bank *

National Westminster Bank

Nationwide-Anglia Building Society

Open University *

Remploy *

Spastics Society *

Trades Union Congress *

* Members of Steering Group

Appendix 2

Types of Disability of People Interviewed

	Number of people with disability interviewed	
Nature of Disability	In open employment	In Remploy
Arthritis		1
Cerebral Palsy		2
Diabetes	1	
Epilepsy		1*
Hearing disability:		
• Non-hearing with speech		1*
• Non-hearing without speech	1	1
• Hearing in one ear	1	
Heart Disease	1	3
Muscular Dystrophy	1	1
Poliomyelitis	1	
Psychiatric and/ or learning disability		6*
Respiratory Condition		3*
Restricted Growth		1
Restricted limb usage	1	2
Skin Condition		1
Spinal Cord Injury	2	1
Visual Disability:		
• Non-sighted	1	
• Partially-sighted	3	1
Total**	13	25

NOTE: *Includes seven people with secondary disabilities in addition to the disability stated above
** Totals include people who were not originally interviewed as having a disability.

Appendix 3

Additional Types of Disability

Those interviewed in open employment organisations reported having experience of managing (Terminology used by interviewees)

Alcoholism

Angina

Anorexia

Bad back

Blackouts

Cancer of the throat

Downs Syndrome

Dyslexia

Haemophilia

Heart attack

High blood pressure

Intestinal problems

Kidney condition

Learning difficulties

Multiple Sclerosis

Parkinson's Disease

Person with one leg

Psychological problems

Someone who walked with sticks

Stress-related illnesses

Thalidomide

Urinary condition

Wheelchair users

Appendix 4

Other Organisations Visited or Consulted

Committees for the Employment of Disabled People
(North West London, North East London and South London)

Department of Employment's Disablement Advisory Service

Greater London Association for Disabled People

IBM

Lambeth ACCORD

Manpower Services Commission

Queen Elizabeth's Training College

London Borough of Camden

London Borough of Lewisham

London Boroughs' Disabilities Resource Team

Rehabilitation Studies Unit, University of Edinburgh

Appendix 5

Profiles of the 'Open Employment' Organisations Researched

Organisation A

Type of business: finance sector. Most jobs are white collar - clerical, administrative, professional, computer or managerial.

Size: interviews carried out at two branches with 7 and 10 staff respectively. These are part of a national network of branches and other offices, with a total staff of approximately 9,000.

Recruitment and selection arrangements: recruitment for clerical jobs is done by local line managers, and for other posts by personnel and line managers. Staff are recruited either for clerical jobs, in head office or branches, or for specialist jobs mainly at head office, or as management trainees.

Management and supervisory training: all in-house, provided at the organisation's training centre, by regional training advisors, and in branches. Core management training consists of three one-week residential courses which include time management, interpersonal skills and assertiveness. Supervisors attend one one-week residential course on first supervisory appointment, covering personal and interpersonal skills. Nomination to attend further residential courses follows appraisal. Most other skills training is carried out at regional and branch level, for example when new products are introduced, and includes the use of distance learning packages and computer-based training.

Disability Policy: A draft equal opportunity policy statement includes reference to disability. No specific guidelines have been issued, but a statement relating to the recruitment of people with disabilities appears in the Personnel Manual, and reference is also made in a staff information booklet. A project team is being set up to look at all equal opportunity issues.

The organisation developed a scheme in 1986, to encourage the recruitment of registered disabled people. Each region, plus head and administrative offices, has two supernumerary posts reserved for registered disabled people, 32 in total (a recent merger has increased this number to 42). Thirty staff (5 male, 25 female) are currently employed on the supernumerary scheme.

Regional managers select the branches to be involved in the scheme. Physical layout as well as attitudes of the staff are taken into account. Branch managers then seek out and select suitable recruits. They are not expected initially to be able to do the full range of tasks expected of trainees, but they should have the potential to do them eventually.

Recruits on the scheme are paid and graded as clerical trainees, and have the normal three month probationary period. After probation, supernumeraries are employed on the same terms and conditions as other staff.

Once they have reached standard performance levels they can be taken on to a manager's staff establishment if a vacancy exists. This has happened with only one of the people recruited under the scheme to date.

Employees with disabilities

Status: on normal terms and conditions.

Numbers: 68 people known of, of whom 48 are registered disabled. Below 1% of total employees including 30 employed as supernumeraries.

Types of jobs: all the supernumeraries and most of the others are in clerical jobs. Three managers known to have developed serious disabilities.

Types of disabilities known to exist: blindness and visual impairment (10 cases), deafness and hearing impairment (6), injury to limbs (6), diabetes (4), back injury (3), cerebral palsy (3), respiratory ailments (3), arthritis (2), epilepsy (2), mental illness (2), multiple sclerosis (2), partial paralysis (2), poliomyelitis (2), spina bifida (2), spinal cord injury (2), amputation, colostomy, cystic fibrosis, muscular dystrophy, bone disease, asthma, gum disease, Crohn's disease, stomach ulcers (1 each).

Training on disability issues for managers and supervisors: no training has any specific disability content, but recruitment training for Branch Managers draws attention to the organisation's recruitment policy in relation to people with disabilities, and a customer care course includes discussion of the needs of customers with disabilities (eg the provision of special interview facilities for those with hearing disabilities).

Role of medical and welfare personnel: All staff working 16 hours or more a week used to have a medical with their own GP on recruitment for admittance to the staff sickness fund. This has recently been replaced by an insurance policy which covers all staff in the event of sickness, and medicals on recruitment are only held if a health problem is mentioned on the application form. Any report from the individual's GP may be sent to the Company GP for comment, but otherwise the information is available only to the Welfare Section. The relevant regional office may be given minimal information which is considered essential for day-to-day management, and which may be passed on to the appropriate branch manager.

Staff with a deteriorating condition may be recruited. Regional and branch managers can refer to the Welfare Section on any disability-related issue.

A GP acts as part-time medical adviser to the Company, carrying out special medical examinations and giving advice, especially when an existing employee develops a serious health problem or becomes disabled.

Organisation B

Type of business: finance sector. Most jobs are white collar - clerical, administrative, sales, professional, computer or managerial.

Size: over 1,000 employees at establishment researched, one of many establishments around the country.

Recruitment and selection arrangements: almost all recruitment done locally, except graduate and specialist recruitment which is national. Several different functional personnel managers do recruiting and shortlisting. Many line managers and supervisors involved in final selection. Much recruitment is for particular job vacancies, but some trainees are recruited for clerical, professional or technical training schemes.

Management and supervisory training: mainly in-house organised either on a Group basis (at more senior levels), or functional level. The organisation, and therefore the training function, is in process of decentralisation, the effects of which are not yet fully worked out. Management and supervisory training not compulsory, except for interviewing training for those involved in graduate recruitment. Few have attended more than one or two week's courses.

Disability Policy: the organisation, in complying with the Companies' Regulations, states that *'It is the Group's policy to give full and fair consideration to applications for employment made by disabled persons, to continue, whenever possible, the employment of staff who become disabled and to provide equal opportunities for the training and career development of disabled employees'.* This has not been translated into any action programme or issuing of guidelines, but an equal opportunities working party is currently considering action in relation to gender, race and disability issues. Equal opportunity committees have been set up within business units.

Employees with disabilities

Status: on normal terms and conditions.

Numbers: unknown, but below quota for registered disabled.

Types of jobs: staff with disabilities in managerial, professional and lower graded jobs.

Types of disabilities known to exist: heart ailments, hearing difficulties and deafness, muscular dystrophy, spinal injury, multiple sclerosis, asthma, cerebral palsy, arthritis, back injuries, epilepsy, diabetes, Parkinson's disease, visual impairment, speech impairment, amputation.

Assessment of staff with fluctuating/deteriorating conditions: carried out by medical staff at the individual's or the line manager's request. Shorter working hours, flexible working and early retirement on favourable terms arranged for some.

Training on disability issues for managers and supervisors: one week course which some have attended, has an input on discrimination, when disability is mentioned. No one in organisation, including personnel staff, thought to have attended any course with any notable disability content.

Role of medical personnel: full-time nursing sisters at three large sites. Part-time doctors make fortnightly visits at the site researched and are available on call. Consultant medical advisors referred to for special cases.

Organisation C

Type of business: public service organisation. Jobs include both white and blue collar, including professional, technical, managerial, administrative, manual and other support staff.

Size: over 2,000 in the head office buildings where most interviews took place. Only central administrative and support staff took part in the study. Many establishments scattered over a wide geographical area, with a total staff of approximately 90,000 over half of whom work part-time.

Recruitment and selection arrangements: most recruitment is carried out centrally, although some has been devolved to three Divisional offices. Selection of teaching staff is carried out by school heads and inspectors jointly. Selection of other professional and support staff is carried out by panels of three, including one line manager, one line staffing officer and one personnel officer. Tests are not normally used except keyboarding skills for clerical staff.

Management and supervisory training: a wide variety provided centrally. Programmes circulated through departmental personnel offices. Staff are nominated by manager or self.

Disability Policy: there is a detailed equal opportunity policy with disability as one aspect. An equal employment opportunities unit within Personnel includes three staff with specific responsibilities for developing and monitoring policies in relation to disability. Following reorganisation, policies have been developed and procedure guidelines have been produced relating to the employment of people with disabilities.

Employees with disabilities

Status: on normal grades, pay and terms and conditions.

Numbers: 205 people known of as being registered disabled (below 1%). Numbers of people with disabilities who are not registered are unknown.

Types of jobs: a wide range including teachers, storekeepers, laboratory technicians, piano tuners, meals supervisors, housefather, other professional and managerial, clerical and administrative.

Types of disabilities known to exist: amputation, arthritis, back injury, blindness and visual impairment, cancer, cerebral palsy, deafness and hearing impairment, diabetes, heart disease, injury to limbs, multiple sclerosis, muscular dystrophy, partial paralysis, poliomyelitis, renal failure, respiratory ailments, spinal cord injury, stroke.

Training for staff with disabilities: clerical and office skills course for deaf and hearing impaired people. Career development course and one-day information seminar held for people with disabilities.

Training on disability issues for managers and supervisors:
- Selection interviewing techniques course includes equal opportunity and disability issues.
- Deaf awareness course for selected managers and colleagues of those who are hearing impaired - 2 days (6 courses held, attended by a total of 50 people).
- Disability and Employment for managers who work with people with disabilities, people in the personnel function and anyone in an advisory role for people with disabilities.
- Seminars are also held for all staff on such subjects as AIDS, alcoholism and stress.

Role of medical and welfare personnel: A staff of full-time and part-time doctors carry out examinations and provide advice. Most have occupational health training. There are also permanent nursing staff, and consultants available on a session basis. Applicants for certain specified jobs, and those over 45, or with a history of severe illness or disability will be examined before recruitment in order to establish whether they are able to do the job.

Existing staff who become disabled or who are returning to work after a sickness absence of more than two months may be seen if they or their manager request it. Medical services may make specific recommendations for changes in hours of work, for example flexible or reduced working is sometimes recommended on full-time pay for a limited period. A scheme for assessment and redeployment used to exist. Its re-establishment would be welcomed, but seems unlikely at present because of financial constraints.

A staff welfare service provides counselling and may also refer an individual to medical services.

Appendix 6

Remploy

Mark Daymond, Director of Personnel at Remploy

Remploy's Background

Towards the end of the war years, the coalition Government of the day began to express concern for the future employment opportunities for those who had suffered severe injuries. Until that time, very little had been done to assist disabled people in finding and retaining jobs. Generally speaking, they were considered unemployable.

Under the chairmanship of Professor Tomlinson, a working party was set up to examine the problem and make recommendations on how to overcome it. The working party established some very important principles (known as the Tomlinson Principles) which are recognised to this day.

The fundamental principles state that:

- there is a national duty to see that those who suffer disablement are given the opportunity of leading as full and useful a life as possible;

- because disablement represents a double loss to the community - a reduction of the total productive capacity and an increase in the cost of maintenance and remedial services - the restoration of a disabled person to productive employment is an economical advantage.

Leading from these accepted principles, a number of proposals were made which the Government then implemented via the 1944 Disabled persons (Employment) Act. Under this Act of Parliament, a number of special provisions were made for severely disabled people, as follows:

- the registration of severely disabled people who are defined in the Act as persons

  'who on account of injury, disease, or congenital deformity are substantially handicapped in obtaining or keeping employment, or in undertaking work on their own account, of a kind which apart from that injury, disease, or deformity would be suited to their age, experience, and qualifications'

- the establishment of a network of Disablement Resettlement Officers across the country

- financial assistance to Local Authorities and certain charitable institutions to provide Sheltered Employment (Sheltered Workshops or Sheltered Placement Schemes)
- setting up a special Government sponsored company - Remploy - which would provide working opportunities throughout Great Britain for severely disabled people, and which would receive financial assistance to enable it to operate.

Remploy was set up to resemble a commercial organisation. The only difference was that it was expected to employ a workforce made up of persons registered as Section 2 - severely disabled people - in return for which the company received annual revenue and capital grants.

Now in its 42nd year, Remploy has become a commercial enterprise of considerable dimensions, mostly in the manufacturing and service sectors of industry. It has 94 factories dispersed across Great Britain, which are organised into 13 trading divisions; these are again sub-divided into about 80 different businesses.

During 1987/88 9,000 severely disabled people were employed, together with 1950 fit people. In 1988/89 the sales income (which covers over two thirds of total company costs) will exceed £100,000,000.

Remploy's Objectives and Employment Policies

Over the years Remploy has established a number of clear objectives and policies which support the nature and purpose of the company. These objectives are set out below:

- to provide productive Sheltered Employment for severely disabled people as defined in Section 15 of the Disabled Persons Employment Act (1944), i.e. Registered Section 2
- within resources available, to employ the maximum number of persons (or number prescribed by the Department of Employment) who are physically, mentally, or visually handicapped in a working environment, who by reason of the nature of severity of their handicap cannot, or are unlikely to, obtain employment in Fit industry and who are willing and able to work
- to provide such employment that will give each person the maximum satisfaction in effort, skill, ability, and reward
- to maintain in each factory a balance and range in terms of disabilities, age, skills, and ability
- to operate the company cost-effectively and efficiently within the limits of its resources, and to achieve economic results which allow Remploy to preserve its image as an industrial organisation, providing

productive employment as opposed to one providing diversionary work, or whose primary function is to assess and train disabled people for ordinary employment.

Disabled people are registered as Section 2 - severely disabled - by DROs (not Remploy). Only Section 2 persons are eligible for sheltered employment. In line with guidelines laid down by the Department of Employment, Remploy expects the output of its disabled people to be maintained at a minimum of 30% of the output of an able-bodied person doing the same or similar work after initial training. Willingness to work and ability of the individual to travel to and from work (financial assistance is provided) are also required.

It will be seen that Remploy is about real work in a real commercially competitive environment. Its output in terms of all aspects of quality must be as good or better than its competitors as it is not permitted to use its subsidy to deliberately undercut its prices.

Remploy therefore offers normality. Normal working disciplines apply, such as an expectation of good time-keeping, willingness to work to the best of one's ability, promotional opportunities, output-related bonus schemes, etc. The company is not about occupational therapy nor is it a charity; it is about real work in a *real* world, thereby demonstrating the truth of the Tomlinson principle which states that *'given the right opportunities, disabled people can, through their work, make a contribution to the Nation's economy.'*

Role of Training in Remploy

Unlike other companies, Remploy does not recruit its workforce (disabled people) in the open labour market. Recruitment is done via DROs, who present a limited number of Section 2 disabled people from which to select. Thus, virtually all recruits are unskilled in the work they will be asked to do; most will have been unemployed for a considerable time; all will have been rejected for work by the rest of commerce and industry.

Remploy Section 2 recruits suffer from a very wide range of physical, nervous, or mental disabilities. Their ability to work both in terms of speed and quality varies greatly - far more so than in fit industry. But the company's job is to identify their abilities and arrange work so these can be used to the best advantage of the individuals and the enterprise. All this requires careful assessment, selection, job placement, job design, performance monitoring and, of course, training. Training may involve more than skill- or job-training; it often includes education in numeracy, literacy, and life skills.

The company is also embarked on promotional training at all levels in the organisation. This is particularly important for disabled employees, whom the company are anxious to promote into supervisory, administrative, or management positions wherever possible. It is no accident that 40% of the company's

600 supervisors were promoted to these positions from originally joining the company as Section 2 hourly paid employees.

Fit manual, administrative, technical, supervisory, and management staff are also recruited. They come from the open job market for specific jobs. Most fit posts, particularly at management level, are advertised internally and externally. On all occasions, the only criteria for selection is capability to do the job. Therefore a Section 2 applicant - if selected for one of these 'fit' posts - is deemed not to require 'sheltered employment.' In this respect, promotion to staff or management posts in Remploy is considered the same as rehabilitation into fit industry.

The company fully recognises its responsibilities for training and development of all its 11,000 employees. Of necessity Remploy has to be labour-intensive. Labour productivity is therefore an essential part of being cost-effective. Machines are also playing an increasingly important role in increasing output and consistent quality of product; computer-assisted machines are opening up new opportunities for disabled people.

In 1984/5, Remploy embarked upon a three-year plan to convert a £7,000,000 trading deficit into a breakeven position. This was called for by the Government. At the same time the revenue grant to Remploy was being reduced in real terms each year. The company had two choices - to meet the target by reducing numbers of employees or by going for substantial growth in sales to produce extra income. It chose the latter and, although a number of 'fit' people had to be made redundant in the process, the number of disabled people actually increased. It is pleasing to record that targets were achieved and surpassed.

It was during this period of growth, which demanded a great deal of everyone in the company, that the results of previous training were fully tested. It also tested supervision and management, where a number of changes had to be made. Over the past five years, over one half of the factory managers and over a quarter of factory supervisors have been newly appointed. This has resulted in quite a reduction in Remploy's line management experience.

To counteract this lack of experience, training programmes in all the usual aspects of supervision and management have been mounted. However, there was a clear need to develop training in Remploy's special dimension - the supervision and management of people suffering from a wide range of disabilities. In the past there had been time for this to be developed over a period of some years' experience. That was no longer possible.

The idea emerged of commissioning two projects to help potential, new, and existing managers and supervisors to carry out their special role in relation to disabled people. These were:

- the development of better assessment techniques to match disabled people to jobs which they could perform satisfactorily;

the development of suitable training for managing and supervising people with severe disabilities.

References

Bolderson H. (1980) The Origins of the Disabled Persons Quota and its Symbolic Significance. *Journal of Social Policy*, Volume 9, No 2, 169-186.

Cornes P. (1982) *Employment Rehabilitation: The Aims and Achievements of a Service for Disabled People*. London: HMSO.

Doyle B. (1987) Employing Disabled Workers: The Framework for Equal Opportunities. *Equal Opportunities Review*, No 12, March April.

Floyd M., Gregory E., Murray H. and Welchman R., (1983) *Schizophrenia and Employment*, London: Tavistock Institute of Human Relations, Occasional Paper No 5.

Kettle M., and Massie B. (1986) *Employers' Guide to Disabilities*. Cambridge: Woodhead Faulkner.

Kulkarni M. R. (1981) *Quota Systems and the Employment of the Handicapped*. Michigan: Michigan University.

Tomlinson Committee (1943) *Report of the Inter-departmental Committee on the Rehabilitation and Resettlement of Disabled Persons*. London: HMSO.

Wansborough N. and Cooper P. (1979) *Open Employment after Mental Illness*. London: Tavistock Press.